THE BOOK OF THE DEAD

The Book of the Dead

MURIEL RUKEYSER

with an introduction by

Catherine Venable Moore

WEST VIRGINIA UNIVERSITY PRESS
MORGANTOWN · 2018

This book has been made possible through a grant from the West Virginia Humanities Council, a state affiliate of the National Endowment for the Humanities.

Copyright © 2018 Muriel Rukeyser
All rights reserved

ISBN:
paper 978-1-946684-21-9

Library of Congress Cataloging-in-Publication Data
is available from the Library of Congress

Book and cover design by Than Saffel / WVU Press

These poems appear in *The Collected Poems of Muriel Rukeyser*, edited
by Janet E. Kaufman and Anne F. Herzog with Jan Heller Levi.
Published in 2005 by the University of Pittsburgh Press.

Catherine Venable Moore's introduction originally appeared in
Oxford American (Fall 2016).

"Shacks and Railroad Tracks in Vanetta" and "George Robinson's
Kitchen in Vanetta" © Estate of Nancy Naumburg Goldsmith,
part of the collection at The Metropolitan Museum of Art.

"Hawk's Nest Dam" and "Portrait of Muriel Rukeyser" © Estate of
Nancy Naumburg Goldsmith.

This volume is dedicated to the hundreds of victims of the Hawk's Nest Tunnel Disaster, both known and unidentified.

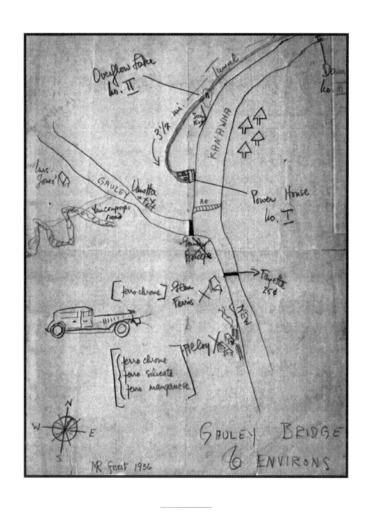

Map of Gauley Bridge and Environs by Muriel Rukeyser, *ca.* 1936.
Courtesy of the Library of Congress.

The Book
of the Dead

By Catherine Venable Moore

*These are roads to take when you think of your country
and interested bring down the maps again*

I was three years old when the Killer Floods hit
West Virginia. We were spared, my family and I. My
parents had recently bought a stone cottage in a
hilly Charleston neighborhood with great schools.
Dad had just graduated from law school. We lost
nothing, while thousands of our neighbors were
ejected from their homes into the icy November
waters that claimed sixty-two lives; the 1985 storms
still sit on the short list of the most costly in U.S.
history. In the aftermath, newspapers accumulated
the miracles and spectacles. An organ caked with
mud, drying before a church. The body of a drowned
deer woven into the under girders of a bridge. Two
nineteenth-century mummies that had floated away

from a museum of curiosities in Philippi, recovered from the river.

None of this suffering was ours. "Ours." My mom—a ginger from the low country whose freckles I was born to—packed me up for a week of relief work in a hangar at the National Guard Armory. Her task was to deal with the hills of black trash bags, sent to Appalachia from abroad, stuffed with clothing that recalled dank basements and dead people's closets. For endless hours, she sorted it into piles by age, size, sex, and degree of suitability. Meanwhile, I dressed up in the gifts of the well-meaning and the careless. Stiletto heels. Crumbling antique hats. Tuxedoes, gowns, belts, and bikinis. "Nobody wants to wear your sweaty old bra, lady," my mom muttered to one of these imagined do-gooders, tossing it aside. On the contrary—I did, very much! I modeled the torn, the stained, and the unusable, cracking up the other volunteers. Mom saw how little of the clothing was functional, how much time was being wasted in the sorting, but she was desperate to be of use.

Disaster binds our people to this place and each other, or so the story goes. Think of the 118 mine disasters our state has suffered since 1894, the fires, explosions, and roof falls. Or the floods, whether "natural"—like the one this June that killed at least twenty-three people (as I write this, my friends come home from recovery work, stinking of contaminated mud)—or those induced by humans, like the coal waste dam that burst at Buffalo Creek in 1972, when 125 people drowned in a tsunami of slurry. (Pittston Coal called it an "act of God.") Other disasters are less visible, inside our bodies even: the rolling crisis that is black lung disease claims a thousand lives every year, while an addiction epidemic seems to be robbing entire generations of our children. West Virginia's drug overdose death rate is the highest in the nation. Then there is the toxic discharge: from the 2014 Elk River chemical spill that poisoned the water of three hundred thousand residents to the micro releases leaking daily from the sediment ponds that serve mountaintop removal sites.

Appalachian fatalism wasn't invented out of thin air. If your list of tragedies gets long enough, you start to think you're fated for disaster. And maybe the rest of the country starts to see you that way, too. I watched a documentary last year about the outsized influence of extractive industries here. It was a well-rehearsed narrative, this litany of disaster—land grab, labor war, boom, bang, roar— on and on in the dark theater. I admired the film in some ways—the bravery of naming each and every pain, the courage of its makers to pass into the tunnel of it, to point fingers along the way. But as I sat through this latest iteration of Appalachian grief writ large, I began to seethe—not at some alleged oppressors, but at the narrative itself. *I cannot live inside the story of this film,* I remember repeating to myself, like a chant. *That can't be my story because nothing lives there.*

Admittedly, there's a spellbinding allure to disaster, close cousin of the sublime. Hypnotic and wordless, the disaster repulses even as it propels one's attention toward it. I know, because I'm victim to its seduction, too. I live five miles from where the Hawk's Nest Tunnel tragedy unfolded, along the New River Gorge in Fayette County. Hawk's Nest is an extreme in a class of extremes—the disaster where truly *nothing* seemed to survive, even in memory—and I have made a home in its catacombs. The historical record is disgracefully neglectful of the event, and only a handful of the workers' names were ever made known. What's more, any understanding of Hawk's Nest involves the discomfort of the acute race divide in West Virginia, seldom acknowledged or discussed. Indeed, race is still downplayed in official accounts. Disaster binds our people, maybe. But what if you're one of those deemed unworthy of memory?

Here's what we know: beginning in June of 1930, three thousand men dug a three-mile hole through a sandstone mountain near the town of Gauley Bridge for the Union Carbide and Carbon Corporation. The

Hawk's Nest Dam.

company was building an electrometallurgical plant nearby, which needed an unlimited supply of power and silica, and the tunnel was determined to be the cheapest and most efficient source of both. A dam would be built to divert a powerful column of the New River underground and down a gradually sloping tunnel to four electrical generators; the ground-up silica rock harvested during excavation would be fed into the furnace in Alloy.

Three-quarters of the workers were migratory blacks from the South who lived in temporary work camps, with no local connections or advocates. Turnover on the job was rapid. By some reports, conditions were so dusty that the workers' drinking water turned white as milk, and the glassy air sliced at their eyes. Some of the men's lungs filled with silica in a matter of weeks, forming scar tissue that would eventually cut off their oxygen supply; others wheezed with silicosis for decades. When stricken, the migrant workers either fled West Virginia for wherever home was, or they were buried as paupers in mass graves in the fields and woods around Fayette County. The death toll was an estimated, though impossible to confirm, 764 persons, making it the worst industrial disaster in U.S. history.

If the company had wet the sandstone while drilling, or if the workers had been given respirators, most deaths would likely have been avoided.

Yet through two major trials, a congressional labor subcommittee hearing in Washington, and eighty-six years of silence, neither Union Carbide nor its contractor—Rinehart & Dennis Company out of Charlottesville, Virginia—has ever admitted wrong-doing. Calling the whole affair a "racket," in 1933 the company issued settlements between $30 and $1,600 to only a fraction of the affected workers and their families. The black workers received substantially less than their white counterparts.

Soon after the project wrapped, the workers' shacks were torn down and a country club built to serve Union Carbide's employees. A state park was established at the site in the mid-1930s, and the Civilian Conservation Corps built a charming stone overlook at what has become one of the most misunderstood and most photographed vistas in the state: the New River, dammed and pooling above the Hawk's Nest Tunnel. Historical memory of the event has since then constituted nothing short of amnesia. Despite its status as the country's "greatest" indus-trial disaster, it remains relatively unknown outside of West Virginia, and even here the incident is barely understood and seldom examined. It took fifty years for the state to mark the deaths at the site. The governor who presided over the disaster's aftermath, Homer Adams Holt, who went on to serve as Union Carbide's general counsel, excised the story from the

WPA's narrative *West Virginia: A Guide to the Mountain State*. Many also believe that when a novel based on Hawk's Nest was published in 1941, Union Carbide convinced Doubleday to pull and destroy all copies.

The word "disaster" emerged from an era when people often aligned fortunes with positions of planetary bodies. It joins the reversing force, "dis-," with the noun for "star." As in, an "ill-fated" misfortune. If a disaster is an imploding star, then the rebirth of a star is its antonym. Recovery is a process of reconstitution—of worldly possessions, of wits. It is never complete. Not today, in the aftermath of June's floods, and not in 1930. Eight decades on, West Virginia hasn't recovered from Hawk's Nest. How could it?—when so much of what was lost still hasn't been named.

Now the photographer unpacks camera and case,
surveying the deep country, follows discovery
viewing on groundglass an inverted image.

I'll admit I've got a thing about falling in love with dead women writers and chasing their ghosts around West Virginia. So when I found out Muriel Rukeyser, an American poet well-known for both her activism and her documentary instincts, had visited and written a famous poem about Hawk's Nest, I had to know more. Rukeyser was born on the eve of World

War I to a well-to-do Jewish family whose heroes, she wrote, were "the Yankee baseball team, the Republican party, and the men who build New York City." Her father co-owned a sand quarry but lost his wealth in the 1929 stock market crash. Until then, it had been a life of brownstones, boardwalks, and chauffeurs. As a girl, she had collected rare stamps with the heads of Bolsheviks and read like mad; slowly, over the course of her childhood, she awakened to what the comforts of her life may have signified in the world.

At twenty-three, Rukeyser found out about the nightmare unfolding in Fayette County from the radical magazines she read, and for which she wrote. After the *New Masses* broke the Hawk's Nest story nationally in 1935, it became the cause célèbre of the New York Left. The House Labor Subcommittee began a hearing on the incident the following January. For a couple of weeks, the country absorbed the event's gruesome details in mainstream media, but the federal government never took up a full investigation, despite the subcommittee's urging. So early in the spring of 1936, Rukeyser and her photographer friend, a petite blonde named Nancy Naumburg, loaded up a car with their equipment and drove from New York to Gauley Bridge to conduct an investigation of their own. I imagine Muriel, fresh from winning the Yale Series of Younger Poets Prize for her first book, *Theory of Flight*, in a smart, fitted blazer and a sensible skirt, glad to take the wheel from Nancy, especially on those curvy roads through the mountains. Their trip would form the foundation of Rukeyser's poem cycle "The Book of the Dead," included in her groundbreaking 1938 collection of documentary poems of witness, *U.S. 1*.

The women originally planned to publish their photographs and text side by side, but for unknown reasons their collaboration never materialized. The method was in vogue at the time, as writers and artists across the country—mostly white—dispatched themselves to document the social ills of the Great Depression in language and film. That same summer of 1936, Margaret Bourke-White and Erskine Caldwell traveled from South Carolina to Arkansas, bearing witness to the Depression's effects on rural communities for what would become *You Have Seen Their Faces*. James Agee and Walker Evans were also traveling, witnessing sharecropper poverty in Alabama for what would become the most famous of these texts, *Let Us Now Praise Famous Men*. The American road guide, as a genre, was also coming into its own. The federal government assigned teams of unemployed writers to turn their ethnographic gaze to the country's landscape and social history, producing the American Guide Series, which aspired to become "the complete, standard, authoritative work on the United States as a whole and of every part of it." The Federal Writers' Project published its first in the Highway Route Guide series, *U.S. One: Maine to Florida,* the same year that Rukeyser released her own *U.S. 1.* "Local images have one kind of reality," she wrote in the endnotes to "The Book of the Dead." "*U.S. 1* will, I hope, have that kind and another too. Poetry can extend the document."

Much of what I know about Rukeyser's life during this period comes, strangely enough, from a 118-page redacted chronicle of her activities, composed by the FBI. In 1943, J. Edgar Hoover authorized his agency to spy on the poet as part of a probe to uncover Russian spies; her "Communistic tendencies" placed her under suspicion of being a "concealed Communist." When the investigation began, she was noted as thirty, "dark," "heavy," with "gray" eyes. In 1933, the report reads, she and some friends drove from New York to Alabama to witness the Scottsboro trial. When local police found them talking to black reporters and holding flyers for a "negro student conference," the police accused the group of "inciting the negroes to insurrections." Then, in the summer of 1936, after her trip to Gauley Bridge, Rukeyser traveled to Spain to report on Barcelona's antifascist People's Olympiad. In the process, she observed the first days of the Spanish Civil War from a train, before evacuating by ship. Her suspicious activities in the 1950s included her appeal for world peace and her civil rights zeal. The FBI mentions "The Book of the Dead" only once, in passing, as a work that dealt with "the industrial disintegration of the peoples in a West Virginia village riddled with silicosis."

Its twenty poems recount the events at Hawk's Nest through slightly edited fragments of victims' congressional testimony, lyric verse, and flashes from Rukeyser's trip south. She lifted her title from a collection of spells assembled to assist the ancient Egyptian dead as they overcame the chaos of the netherworld—"that which does not exist"—so they could be reborn. One of these texts, which concerns the survival of the heart after death, was carved onto the back of an amulet called the Heart Scarab of Hatnefer, a gold-chained stone beetle pendant that the Metropolitan Museum of Art excavated from a tomb and put on display in New York in 1936, the same year Rukeyser began her version of "The Book of the Dead."

Curious to learn more about Rukeyser's time in West Virginia, I called up a scholar named Tim Dayton, who had searched the poet's papers for clues about the poem's composition. He told me that Naumburg's glass plate negatives of Gauley Bridge have since been lost, and that Rukeyser's research notes are missing. The only evidence of their journey, I learned, consisted of a letter, a map, and Rukeyser's treatment for a film called "Gauley Bridge," published in the summer 1940 issue of *Films,* but never produced.

In the letter dated April 6, 1937, Naumburg offered Rukeyser her "personal reactions to Gauley Bridge" and suggested a general outline for the piece. The document provides some clues about whom the women spoke to and what they saw—a few names, a vignette or two, and a description of the "miserable conditions" of those living with silicosis. "Show how the tunnel itself is a splendid thing to look at, but a terrible thing to contemplate," Nancy wrote to her friend. Show "how the whole thing is a terrible indictment of capitalism." She signed off, "Are you going to the modern museum showing tomorrow nite?"

The map of "Gauley Bridge & Environs" is signed by Rukeyser and drawn in her hand. At the center is the confluence of the New and Gauley rivers, where they form the Kanawha. Off to the side she sketched their little car, its headlights beaming forward. In cartoonish simplicity, she outlined the shapes that I recognize from my daily life: the trees, the bridge, Route 60. But some of her markings held greater mystery: a long, winding road jutting back into the mountains labeled, as best I could make out, "Nincompoop's Road"; a house that was "Mrs. Jones'." Rukeyser marked a big X on the town of Gauley Bridge, and an X over Alloy, rendered as a boxy factory belching smoke. She drew clusters of Xs next to two towns

I'd never heard of on the Gauley River: Vanetta and Gamoca. This tracing of my home in her hand held the promise of a new way of knowing Hawk's Nest.

I gradually came to see that "The Book of the Dead" is itself a kind of map. (So much so that a literary critic, Catherine Gander, convincingly argues for the text to be read as a rhizomatic map in the spirit of Deleuze and Guattari's *A Thousand Plateaus*.) Not only do the poems' titles quite literally refer to people's names and elements of the landscape—"The Road" or "The Face of the Dam: Vivian Jones"—the sequence also sketches out a crucial yet missing piece of the official Hawk's Nest story, a narrative thread usually so common in the media's treatment of disaster that it's become a trope: the "pulling together of community." Six poems in, we meet the Gauley Bridge Committee, an organized group of ten tunnel victims, their family members, and witnesses, whose caretaking and advocacy role had been totally absent from anything I'd read about the crisis up to that point.

Rukeyser introduces them in "Praise of the Committee." They sit around a stove under a single bare bulb, in the back of a shoe repair shop in Gauley Bridge, amid the din of machine belts. They are: Mrs. Leek (*cook for the bus cafeteria*); Mrs. Jones (*three lost sons, husband sick*); George Robinson (*leader and voice*); four other black workers (*three drills, one camp-boy*); Mearl Blankenship (*the thin friendly* man); Peyton (*the engineer*); Juanita (*absent, the one outsider member*).

The room is packed with tunnel workers and their wives, waiting. The Committee's purpose is to feed and clothe the sick and lobby for legislation. George Robinson calls the meeting to order. They discuss the ongoing lawsuits, a bill under consideration, the relief situation. They talk about Fayette County Sheriff C. A. Conley, owner of the hotel in town, who heads up "the town ring." Rumor has it that he's intercepting parcels of money and clothing at the post office, sent by well-meaning New Yorkers to tunnel victims. At the end of the poem, their spectral voices rise up like the chorus from a classical tragedy, asking: *Who runs through electric wires? Who speaks down every road?*

This scene played over and over in my head like the beginning of a film I wanted to believe existed about Hawk's Nest. A film like the one Muriel meant to make, a story of dignity and resistance that was yet to be told.

Touch West Virginia where

the Midland Trail leaves the Virginia furnace,
iron Clifton Forge, Covington iron, goes down
into the wealthy valley, resorts, the chalk hotel.

Pillars and fairway; spa; White Sulphur Springs.

In the early Appalachian spring of this year—what proved to be the wet eve of June's storms—I found myself barreling down Route 60 with "The Book of the Dead" in the passenger's seat. The rivers swelled brown and bristled with snags of trees beneath color-drained mountains capped with a dusting of snow. I was following Rukeyser's map, becoming a tourist in my own home. Along the road I saw metal buildings printed with soda pop logos and heard the shrieks of peepers in their vernal ponds. Easter loomed, and a church's sign assured me: DEATH IS DEFEATED. VICTORY IS WON.

First stop: the "wealthy valley" from the cycle's opening poem, White Sulphur Springs. It began as a resort hotel, marketing the area's geothermal springs and relative freedom from insect-borne disease to slaveholding autocrats across the South, who evacuated their families from the lowlands each summer. The hotel was known then as the Old White—a string of cottages encircling a bathhouse, where the South's antebellum politics and fashions played out around a burble of sulfurous waters with allegedly curative properties. Later owners the C&O Railroad changed the name to the Greenbrier. Though the sickly smelling spring was capped in the 1980s, the hotel is still run as a resort with a casino by West Virginia's current governor, the coal operator Jim Justice.

Whenever I catch sight of the Greenbrier, there's an initial moment of nausea. Like standing in the center of a vast array of radio telescopes or driving up a holler surrounded by a massive but out-of-sight surface mine. When Rukeyser drove through, the hotel's stark white façade had just been redone, but the inside was still Edwardian and dim, draped in the depressing purples and greens of a deep bruise. Global merchant powerhouses like the du Ponts and the Astors would have been flying into the brand-new airport for the hotel's famous Easter celebration, where princesses, movie stars, and politicians performed their circus of white gentility.

I parked beside a utility van brimming with roses and entered the building's interior galleries, which glowed like Jell-O–colored jewels. A dramatically lit hallway displayed busts of what appeared to be the same white man carved over and over in alabaster. I watched as workers prepared for daily tea service by putting out plates of sweets, around which tourists swarmed like wasps. A cheeky pianist played the theme song to *Downton Abbey* as I grabbed a cookie and made my way back outside. I wandered down Main Street to Route 60 American Grill and Bar, where a man from Jamaica was beating a man from Egypt at pool. The bartender answered the ringing phone: "Route 60, may I help you?" Chunks of something slid into the fryer. I played "I Saw the Light" on the jukebox and drank by myself, before heading off to sleep in my car at the Amtrak station, a redbrick cottage perpetually decorated for Christmas. The entire town of White Sulphur Springs would in a few months be under floodwaters; three bodies would be pulled from the resort grounds, where the five golf courses had, in a handful of hours, become a lake.

The next morning, I continued along the path Rukeyser laid out in her poem "The Road," rolling westward through the Little Levels of the Greenbrier Valley, passing limestone quarries and white farmhouses drifting in pools of new, raw grass. In Rainelle, I stopped at Alfredo's to eat an eggplant sandwich in a room full of steelworkers talking about ramps, the garlicky onion that heralds our spring. After, I skirted the mangled guardrails of Sewell Mountain, a 3,200-foot summit that today is clear-cut by loggers, where Gen. Robert E. Lee once headquartered himself under a sugar maple in the fall of 1861. I passed Spy Rock, where Native Americans sent up signal fires, watched for their enemies. New beech leaves glistered like barely hardened films.

In the afternoon, I arrived at the Reconstruction-era courthouse in Fayetteville, less than one mile from my home, and climbed its entrance of pink sandstone. Most tunnel-related court documents were turned over to Rinehart & Dennis as part of the 1933 settlement deal. Even so, I found overlooked summonses, pleas, and depositions scattered throughout the county's hundreds of case files. Soon, I held a blueprint of the tunnel in my hands, apparently entered as an exhibit in the first case to go to trial. It suggested the elegance of a graphic musical score yet filled me with that stony disaster dread. At the time of the trial, some of the plaintiff's witnesses were actively dying. Still, the jury deadlocked, and accusations of jury tampering arose when one juror was observed traveling to and from the courthouse in a company car. In time, the plaintiff's lawyers were on record for having accepted a secret payment of $20,000 from Rinehart & Dennis to grease the wheels for a settlement. (In a turn of unexpected, though slight, justice, half the money was later distributed among their clients, by judge's order.)

As I sat in the clerk's office trying to put the pieces together, Fayette County Circuit Judge John Hatcher walked in. We traded wisecracks back and forth for a while, and then I showed him what I was looking at. "Awful what happened," Hatcher said. "They killed a lot of blacks." Then he launched into a story from World War II in which the American GIs gave out chocolate bars to the survivors of a concentration camp, but the richness of the sweets made their starving bodies sick. I wasn't sure what the point of his story was until he looked me square in the eyes and said: "Nazis."

I am a Married Man and have a family.   God
knows if they can do anything for me
it will be appreciated
if you can do anything for me
let me know soon

I left Fayetteville and followed Route 60 over Gauley
Mountain, crossing the tunnel's path three times. I
came into Gauley Bridge, the first community off
the mountain and the first one you come to on
Rukeyser's map. It's equal parts bucolic river town and
postindustrial shell. I stopped at a thrift store, one of
the only open businesses in the downtown core, and
bought a copy of Conley and Stutler's *West Virginia
Yesterday and Today* for thirty-five cents. Adopted
officially into the public school curriculum in 1958 but
used widely in classrooms since its publication in 1931,
it's literally a textbook case of white people's amnesia.
The index does not list "Slavery." The existence of
"Negroes" is acknowledged six times, most often in
relation to their "education." It's mute on the lost lives
at Hawk's Nest, offering instead a description of an
engineering marvel and a scenic overlook.

    Back out on the street, I heard a sweet voice call
out: "Diamond, are you working today?" I looked up
and saw a frail man with pale blue eyes, rubbing his
nose with a tissue. I told him I was Catherine but
that I wished my name were Diamond, and he said,

"You favor her. She just started working down at the nursing home."

He turned out to be Pastor Charles Blankenship, the preacher at Brownsville Holiness Church and the proprietor of the New River Lodge, formerly the Conley Hotel, where I planned to stay the night. What looked to me now like three shabby stories of grayish-yellow brick was a swanky stop for travelers when it was built in 1932, something I could imagine on the backstreets of Miami Beach. I believed Charles when he told me that Hank Williams had stayed at the Conley on many occasions. There's strong evidence that Rukeyser had stayed here too; her son Bill remembers a black-and-white postcard of it among her keepsakes.

In 2016, I found the lobby a friendly clutter of dusty MoonPies, hurricane lamps, and old panoramic photos that lit up for me the Gauley Bridge of 1936: its busy bus station and café, its theater and filling stations, the scenes of prior floods. A bulletin board displayed one of those optical illusions of Jesus with his eyes closed—stare at it long enough (i.e., *believe*), and his eyes are supposed to open. Most of the hotel's residents today are long-term tenants, elderly or on housing assistance, but this lobby used to hum, Charles told me, recalling the thick steaks that fried on the grill at the restaurant. The Conley filled up most nights when Charles's

Shacks and Railroad Tracks in Vanetta.

dad worked here as a porter, hauling luggage to the rooms of rich people passing through on their way to the East Coast. "I can picture them coming through the door," Charles said. "He used to get calls all night."

Charles was born in 1939 and grew up in a company house in a nearby coal camp called Big Creek, located about where Rukeyser drew "Nincompoop's Road" on her map. Like everyone I would meet, he wanted to know what I was doing in Gauley Bridge, so I told him I was looking into Hawk's Nest and Rukeyser's poem. He said he preached a funeral a few years ago for a woman whose daddy died of silicosis in the tunnel. He mentioned this fact in his sermon, and after the service, some of the woman's relatives came up and thanked him. They hadn't known.

I suddenly thought of the cycle's poem titled "Mearl Blankenship," about a "thin friendly man" who worked on the tunnel and served on the Gauley Bridge Committee. I asked Charles whether he had any relatives by that name. "That was my daddy," he said. I told him about Nancy's letter to Muriel, in which she wrote, "Stress, through the stor[y] of Blankenship . . . the necessity of a thorough investigation in order to indict the Co., its lawyers and doctors and undertaker, how the company cheated these menout [*sic*] of their lives."

"Well, what about that?" asked Charles with wonder. "He possibly did. . . ." He told me that his dad, whose nickname was Windy, had died at the age of forty-one. "He took that heart attack right over there," Charles said, gesturing toward some couches in the lobby. That night his father had told Sheriff Conley, the hotel owner, over and over: "I'm hurting so bad in my chest." Through the night, Conley fed him an entire bottle of aspirin pills. By the time he was rushed to a medical clinic around 2 a.m., Mearl had just hours to live.

I read "Mearl Blankenship" to Charles. Most of it consists of a letter that "Mearl," a steel nipper who laid track in the tunnel, wrote to a newspaper in the city about his condition. At that point, he was losing weight and feared the worst. When I got through reading the poem, Charles said: "That wouldn't be my dad. He never worked like that over there." I asked him who he thought the guy in the poem was, and he said he didn't have a clue. "It's very unusual because all the Blankenships I knew." He asked me for a photocopy, and then we discussed the brand-new aorta he got for free from a hospital in Cleveland.

That evening, I attended Charles's church with a friend. The sanctuary of Brownsville Holiness, perched on a pitched hillside along the Gauley River, is adorned with red wall-to-wall carpet and a single, simple wooden cross. Services kicked off

George Robinson's Kitchen in Vanetta.

with an hour's worth of live karaoke for the Lord, as congregants took turns singing at the altar, backed by members of a band who arrived late and casually set up around them. Then they all prayed in tongues. After, Charles shouted, "To know Christ is like coming out of a dark tunnel into the light! There is power in the blood of the Lamb! In the city where the Lamb is the light, you won't need no electric there!" On multiple occasions, he stopped the service cold and asked both my Jewish companion and myself to approach the altar and give witness. I smiled with a Presbyterian's customary politeness and declined. "Maybe next time," said my good-natured friend.

Brother Nathan, with his thin, tawny hair and slow, easy voice, rose to read a scene from scripture. Simon and the other disciples were gathering up their fishing nets after nary a nibble all night, just as Jesus told them to throw the nets back out again, for no apparent reason. "Nevertheless," said Simon, "at thy word I will let down the net." Brother Nathan told us, "The facts will scare you. We need to put aside the facts. It's time to say, 'Nevertheless.' I don't care what the enemy throws at me. The devil can come at me every which way, but nevertheless, I'm going on with God, I'm going on with God, and I'm going all the way. . . . Nevertheless, nevertheless, nevertheless . . ."

Weeks later, I still wished I'd gone to the altar, that I'd known the right words about the tunnel to take there. Instead, I pieced together a Mearl Blankenship from census records—a white baby born "Orin M" in 1908 in the lumber company camp called Swiss. Ten years later, the family was farming; in 1930, "Murrell" was twenty-one and literate, living with his parents in the Falls district of Fayette among coal miners, dam construction laborers, painters, lumber ticks, and dairy farmers. By 1940, ten years after tunnel construction began, "Myal" was an unemployed cement mixer, married to Clara, with whom he had three children, including an infant, Charles. He worked only twenty weeks in 1939 and earned $800. He died of a heart attack on February 3, 1950, and was buried at Line Creek. Charles was ten years old.

I brought a copy of "Mearl Blankenship" back to the Conley on a cold spring day several weeks after my initial visit to Gauley Bridge—"a rough old day," as Pastor Charles put it. I found him eating cheese puffs out of a coffee filter in the dim hotel lobby. He welcomed me back, took the poem, and this time, read it to himself silently. He finally looked up, tearful, and said, "I'd say that was my Dad. I had no idea. It stands to reason he worked there, because there was no other work back then."

What Charles remembered of his father was his sleeping body glimpsed through the doorway of their coal camp house. Light filtered through some kind of sheer curtain. Once, Charles watched a black snake slither out of the ceiling and dangle in midair over Mearl as he slept. Charles repeated the story about Sheriff Conley and the bottle of aspirin. He repeated the story about the family who didn't know that their kin worked at Hawk's Nest. When I finally got up to leave, he held my hand tight, locked into my gaze, and told me that he loved me. I told him I loved him back.

George Robinson holds all their strength together:
To fight the companies   to make somehow a future.

"At any rate, it is inadvisable to keep a community of dying persons intact."

While reporting this story, I learned that two of Nancy Naumburg's photos from Gauley Bridge had resurfaced at the Metropolitan Museum of Art. The first is a shot of a town where black tunnel workers lived, Vanetta, which Rukeyser had marked with a cluster of Xs on her map. Raw wood structures line a thin strip of land between the railroad and the Gauley River. The air holds fog—or is it smoke? A scatter of people sits waiting for a train in the distance, where the tracks vanish into perspective.

After my first night at the Conley, I woke early and started down the abandoned rail line toward Vanetta. The cool, misty air sang with the frenzy of mating frogs and feeding birds. A dripping rock wall rose up on my right; wild blue phlox, oyster mushrooms, and sandy beaches spread down to the river on my left. After crossing a trestle, I began to pass into the frame of Nancy's photograph.

It was the same bend in the track that Leon Brewer, a statistician with the Federal Emergency Relief Administration, rounded in 1934. The apocalyptic dispatch he filed in confidence soon afterward counted 101 residents of Vanetta, occupying "41 tumble-down hovels, [with] 14 children, 44 adult females, and 43 adult males." All but ten of the men were sick. "Support for the community comes from the earnings of 15 of the males, 14 of whom suffer from silicosis. Thirteen are engaged on a road construction project 18 miles away and are forced to walk to and from work, leaving them but 5 hours a day for labor. Moreover many . . . are frequently too weak to lift a sledge hammer."

According to Brewer, these black families froze through the winter, starved and begged for both food and work. (One white local told me that he used to hunt for duck in the area where some of the sick, hungry workers camped on flat rocks next to the river; once, they asked him to bring them back a duck, and instead he returned with crow as a joke.) Brewer called for direct relief, "despite the protests of the white people," and an immediate improvement in housing and sanitation. He declared that anyone who wanted to return home should be given passage and assistance with reconnecting to his or her home community. "At any rate," he wrote, "it is inadvisable socially to keep a community of dying persons intact. Every means should be exerted to move these families, so that they may be in communities where they will be accepted, and where the wives and children will find adjustment easier."

The other Naumburg image that resurfaced depicts the interior of a worker's home in Vanetta: George Robinson's kitchen. Robinson, who came from Georgia, was the closest thing to a media spokesperson that the black tunnel worker ever had. In the frame of the photo, light falls onto a cookstove with kettles at the ready, the papered-over wall of Robinson's board-and-batten home arrayed with essential cooking implements: a whisk, a muffin tin, a roasting pan. A white rag dries on a line in the light.

I conjure the scene in the shack. I see George sitting, reciting what he told Congress and the juries, almost rote by now. His breathing is labored. I see his wife, Mary—is she distracted by thoughts of dinner, whether she should offer these women something to eat? Has a white lady ever been in her kitchen? Maybe they reminded her of the social workers who came from Gauley Bridge. Maybe Nancy is setting up her camera, her head ducking under the black cloth, as she peers through the ground glass, trying to get the focus right. Why, Mary wonders, had she chosen that wall? What did she read there? Did Mary want it to be read? Muriel sits, jotting down what George tells her in a notebook, wanting to capture it all, but also attempting to maintain eye contact—aware at every moment of the discomfort her privilege brings into the room. Was theirs a welcome visit, I wonder, or did the presence of these two white women disrupt the family's hard-won and precarious sense of sanctuary?

Muriel and Nancy made this visit in the spring that followed Robinson's congressional testimony; by June he was in the hospital, and by July 1 he was dead of "Heart Trouble" at fifty-one. On July 12, they buried him at Vanetta. I never found George Robinson on any census, nor do I know if he had children, or where I might begin to search for any surviving relatives. The only picture of him I ever came across was an Acme press photo from the D.C. hearing in which he is misidentified in the caption as "Arthur" (for that matter, his last name was misspelled in the congressional record). He sits at a table with papers spread around him, wearing a plaid woolen coat and button-up shirt. His arm is raised mid-gesture and his mouth paused mid-speech as he describes to the labor subcommittee chair the conditions under which he worked and contracted silicosis.

Robinson testified that he ran a sinker drill straight down into the rock, that it was operated dry, and that he wasn't given any protective gear. He witnessed two men crushed by falling rock. "The boss was always telling us to 'hurry, hurry, hurry,'" he said. He described the dusty trees in the labor camps where black workers lived around the tunnel mouth, the shack rousters paid by the company to physically coerce the sick men to work. Sheriff Conley came around and ran off those who couldn't continue, he said, men so weak they had to "stand up at the sides of trees to hold themselves up." He remembered one who died under a rock. Robinson knew of 118 who perished, had personally helped bury thirty-five, and estimated a total death toll of five hundred. He said the company burned down the camps when the project was complete, so the workers would scatter. They even "put some of the men in jail because they wouldn't vacate the houses."

Bernard Jones—a white man who lost his father, uncle, and three brothers to silicosis—gave new context to this exodus story in a 1984 oral history with occupational health specialist Dr. Martin Cherniack. The white merchants at Gauley Bridge had liked the idea of the tunnel workers at first, said Jones, because they thought money was to be made from them. But eventually, they got "irritated" and accused them of "thieving," stockpiling stolen goods under a nearby railroad bridge. The merchants and professionals wrote an open letter denouncing the media for printing "propaganda" about their town, decrying the "undesirables, mainly Negroes" who had taken up residence there. Still, some of the black workers who lacked either the health or the means to go elsewhere attempted to stay in Vanetta.

"Who it was I do not know," said Bernard, "but somebody in Gauley Bridge went across the river in Vanetta, and they put a big cross up there on the hillside and wrapped it with rags and soaked it with gasoline and set it on fire. Well, these black people, when they seen that cross burning, that scared them. And the next morning one group right after another came down that railroad track headed for the bus station, going back home to the South."

And now here I was, the latest white witness-invader, tromping in the opposite direction, back into Vanetta, where not a single structure was left. I saw a path that led from the tracks up the hillside and into the woods. Rukeyser's poem "George Robinson: Blues" tells me to look to the hills for the graveyard, and so I followed its lines into what was becoming a warm, cloudless spring day. I found it: a cemetery covering the whole mountain. I saw a corroded gravestone from 1865 and the fresh grave of an infant buried the day before, but I never found George Robinson's.

He shall not be diminished, never;
I shall give a mouth to my son.

In press photos and newsreels from 1936, Emma
Jones appeared white, beautiful, and hungry.
Sometimes she wore a little fur around her neck. She—
who had lost three sons and was soon to lose both her
brother and her husband—had become the white face
of the tunnel's suffering in the American mind, the
media's "Migrant Mother" of this particular disaster.

When construction began, she and her husband,
Charley, lived at Gamoca (Jah-MO-kah), an unin-
corporated community with a company store and a
swinging bridge over the river, just down the tracks
from Vanetta. She had nine children at the time
and would go on to have two more. Charley and her
sons worked in the coal mines, when there *was* work
(which there wasn't). That is to say, they bootlegged.
It was one of Charley's customers, a foreman at
the tunnel, who convinced them to look for jobs at
Hawk's Nest. Charley became a water boy. Cecil, the
oldest son, was a driller. The youngest, Shirley, a
nipper. And Owen, the middle son, had a mean streak
and disliked blacks, so the company supervisors
made him a foreman and gave him a ball bat.

The brothers got sick around the same time; their
father held out a few years longer. Emma went out
to Route 60 and begged for money to buy them chest

X-rays. Before Shirley died—so skeletal Emma could lift and move him around the house like a lamp—he made his mother promise to have the family doctor perform an autopsy on his body. The doctor, in fact, preserved the lungs of all three brothers, hardened like cement, in jars as proof of their disease. *The Jones Boys.* That's what the doctor's son and his wife called the disembodied lungs after the old doctor died, I guess to make the whole thing feel less atrocious. The lungs sat in the couple's basement for years like forgotten pickles—until they loaded them into the back of their pickup truck, drove them up to the dump at the top of Cotton Hill Mountain, and chucked them over the side. "They sure made a racket when they went down over the mountain," the doctor's wife said later in an oral history, "but it sounded like just one jar broke." I used to live on the back side of Cotton Hill and spent long summer afternoons searching for the jars, to no avail. I imagined the ghost lungs fluttering through the forest at night like little sets of wings, surrounded by halations of shimmering silica dust.

I learned that many of the Jones family's descendants still lived in the area. People like Anita Jones Cecil, one of Charley and Emma's grandchildren. I hesitated before contacting her, worried that I would disrupt her grieving process, or that she wouldn't want to talk to me; worse yet, that she'd want me to stop talking. But when I found her on Facebook one day, it seemed like maybe she'd been waiting awhile to tell this story. "My family is chained to that place by ghosts," she wrote in the message box. "Hawk's Nest chained my grandmother and my father to Fayette County through generational poverty. . . . I have three sisters and two brothers, and I am the only one that went to college. We didn't have a chance."

Anita agreed to meet up at the library in downtown Charleston, where we settled next to a window in a dim, empty meeting room. She struck me as graceful and strong, with long brown hair and brown eyes, deep dimples, and a gaze that felt like a steady hand. She said, "This is what my dad told me, and what I actually think: they actively sought people who were poor, who were desperate and uneducated, and shipped them up here. Expendable people. People that nobody would miss."

Together, we looked at Rukeyser's map. I pointed out the house labeled "Mrs. Jones'." Anita told me it was the small farm that Emma and Charley bought for $1,700 with their settlement money, near present-day Brownsville Holiness. They received roughly twice the compensation that a black family would have received, but there was still nothing leftover to live on, and Charley had to go back to work in the coal mines to pay off their debts. For a short time, while she was pregnant with Wilford (Anita's father), Emma worked at a WPA sewing factory in Gauley Bridge to support the family. Her oldest surviving son later said that she gave away bags of potatoes and flour to needy neighbors until the money ran out, and the family was right back where they started.

Charley died in 1941, leaving Emma a single mother with three children under eighteen. Then their house burned down. Emma turned to the Holy Spirit to get her through those times—she prayed and spoke in tongues. Eventually, she remarried and settled in a four-room coal camp house in Jodie, and life got a little easier. She had one of the nicest homes in town, with red tar shingles, a little fishpond, and a colony of elephant ears that she grew and shared with her neighbors. Anita may have never met her grandmother, but she grew up in that house, raised by her grandmother's ghost.

Anita said her father used to warn her not to depend on anybody else, not even a man, for anything. "You have to make it on your own"—that's what the tunnel taught Wilford Jones. But Anita thought it taught him something else, too. "My dad was always going on and on about how you should treat everybody the same, everybody's equal no matter what the race, religion, any of that kind of stuff. And I think that was directly related to his experiences as a little child." Anita said her father was clever, could do math in his head. He started college but couldn't figure out a way to pay for it, so he came home to help support the family. The only work he could find was in the coal mines, and by the time Anita was a child, he was sick with black lung. She told me it didn't hold him back. Once, while he healed from heart surgery, "The miners went on strike, and he wanted to go out and picket with staples in his chest," she said. "That's the kind of people we're dealing with when you talk about my family." Near the end, perhaps delirious from lack of oxygen, Wilford got the idea that he was the actual son of Mother Jones, the union organizer who radicalized after she lost her four sons and husband to yellow fever. Some people had a theory that she had given her children up instead, to shield them from the dangers of her work. It became part of Wilford's truth that he was one of those sacrificed sons. Before he died at the age of fifty-six, he told his family to open his chest when he was gone, just as they'd done to his brothers, to perform an autopsy and prove he had black lung. He told them to seek compensation. "I think he dwelled on the past and thought about how things should have been and was sad over it," said Anita. "I personally, I'm a little bit mad."

Anita channeled that rage into a career in social services—she became an economic service worker at the West Virginia Division of Rehabilitation Services, processing relief applications and determining eligibility for Social Security and SSI. When Anita drives past the Alloy plant today, she thinks, "That's who killed my family. That's where our lives went. . . . I watch it happen over and over again in West Virginia, where families of coal miners, families of Hawk's Nest, will lose their primary breadwinner and they just struggle and struggle and struggle until they die." After all the death, after all the wealth was shipped out of the tunnel, she said, nothing was ever given back to Gauley Bridge—no investment in education or infrastructure. "Instead of being developed, it died with those men."

We read Rukeyser's poem "Absalom" together, facing each other in two chairs before a window overlooking the main intersection of Charleston's modest downtown. Somewhere in the shadows of the room, I like to think Muriel was there—her wavy hair pushed back from her wide forehead, a dimple marking her soft chin. Anita held a photocopy of the poem in her hands, while I held the recorder. She leaned forward, reading half silently and half out loud lines from her grandmother's congressional testimony, jump cut with fragments of spells from *The Egyptian Book of the Dead*. When Anita got to lines that interested her, she stopped and free-associated.

One of these was a passage that Rukeyser appropriated from the ancient text, meant to ensure that the hearts of the deceased were given back to them before rebirth. Then the deceased get their mouths back, and their limbs stretch out with an electrical charge. They are reembodied, with the power to move between portals of worlds freely. "I will be in the sky . . ." the dead chant.

I asked Anita where she found hope in this story—her story, any of them—because sometimes I simply could not. She said, "Have you ever really looked at Gauley Mountain, how beautiful it is? That's where I find my hope, yes. You think to yourself, God's here. He's here. He's not forgotten any one of those souls that died." She handed me a Bible verse she'd written out: "Fear not, therefore, for there is nothing covered that shall not be revealed; nothing hidden that shall not be known."

"That's what I think of when I think of Hawk's Nest," Anita said. "I'm not afraid. 'Cause I know everything will come out eventually."

I take her to mean, "God knows what that company did."

A few weeks later, I walked three-abreast on the train tracks with Anita and Rita Jones Hanshaw, Anita's sister, toward Gamoca Cemetery, where most of the Jones family is buried. The day threatened rain; the Gauley flowed deep and brown in flood, though we were still months from the June storms that would bury Belva in water. The sisters debated the way up to the graves. Anita tore through the thickening understory in one direction, while

Rita and I started up a rugged logging path. Both women found it at once: the array of bathtub-size depressions in the earth, clusters of metal markers nestled among saplings, with blank spaces where the names once were. Tree roots heaved up and twisted the iron fences encircling the burial plots. We came to a slight clearing, shaded by giant hemlock and carpeted in Easter lilies—there in a row, Shirley, Cecil, Owen, and Charley lay buried. A family member with money had recently invested in flat stone markers, engraved with their names. Emma's body rests with her second family in nearby London, West Virginia.

Rita, the spitting image of her grandmother, spoke of her thirst for justice; of Shirley, who was working in the tunnel to save money for college; the thrill she felt a few years ago when she first heard the sound of her grandfather's voice, caught in an old newsreel someone posted on YouTube. Around that time, she and her sister Tammy began digging in the archives for the death certificates of tunnel workers, as a kind of self-fashioned therapy. "We just feel that us doing the research, and finding out what happened, it helps us heal. I know it was before we were born, but we still have feelings about this. It's our grandparents, people we didn't get to know. And through this we feel like we're growing to know them."

For those given to voyages : these roads
discover gullies, invade, Where does it go now?
Now turn upstream twenty-five yards. Now road again.
Ask the man on the road. Saying, That cornfield?

The white cemeteries wouldn't accept the growing number of black dead, and the slave graveyard at Summersville was already full. So Union Carbide paid an undertaker named H. C. White $55 for each tunnel worker he buried in a field on his mother's farm in neighboring Nicholas County. In 1935, a photo of cornstalks and mass graves on the White Farm made its way into the mainstream press and eventually caught the concern of a congressman from New York, who called for an inquiry into the accusations of corporate criminality at Hawk's Nest. Members of the Gauley Bridge Committee and others gave nine days' worth of official testimony, but Congress never took up the labor subcommittee's recommendation to investigate. (The West Virginia legislature passed a weak silicosis statute in 1935, essentially set up to protect employers from similar future disasters.) Nevertheless, a trove of eyewitness and victims' accounts, which would have otherwise gone missing, had been put down on record. And without that, it's hard to imagine Rukeyser's "Book of the Dead"—or much of any memory at all.

The White family sold their farm in 1954, and the record remained more or less as it was until 1972. That year, the state surveyed for a new four-lane road and found human remains in its path, sixty-three possible graves. A state contractor sifted through the soil for bones and placed them in three-foot boxes, reburying them adjacent to the highway, along the towering pink sandstone cliffs that edge Summersville Lake. H. C. White's son, the local undertaker of record, signed off on the whole thing. And there they remained, forgotten again, until 2012.

Thirty miles from Gamoca, at a highway exit called Whippoorwill, I met up with Charlotte Yeager, who played a role in the recent rediscovery of the Hawk's Nest burials. I parked next to a guardrail strewn with the Weed-Eaten heads of wild daisies. Charlotte, the publisher of the *Nicholas Chronicle,* emerged from a gray minivan with a pin on her chest in the shape of a ramp. It was April, and Richwood (another town hit hard by the June floods) had just hosted its big feed.

Charlotte heard the rumors about the bodies of black workers buried in the hills when she moved from Charleston to Summersville twenty years ago. "Everybody knew it, you know. It was just kept hush-hush because they were embarrassed." She tried a few times to locate them but with no luck. Then one day, she read a story in the Charleston paper about two guys—likewise haunted by the missing men—who had led a reporter to this site, claiming it held some of the workers' graves. One of them, Richard Hartman, later told me that the first time he went to Whippoorwill, he had to pick his way over rusting appliances and piles of roadkill that the highway department had been tossing over the side of the road for years. The sun's glint on a metal grave marker between the trees and trash was all that gave it away.

After that newspaper story, word got out, and a group of community members arose around a common desire to rededicate the cemetery. They included not only Charlotte, but local high school students, religious leaders, filmmakers, government officials, and descendants of white tunnel victims— like the Joneses. They cleared the area around the graves; the state came out and did a radar survey of the site. Rita Jones Hanshaw, a schoolteacher, and her sister Tammy began digging into vital records for names of workers. Plans for a memorial park were drawn up and then realized at a 2012 ceremony honoring the dead. A white barefoot preacher from Summersville joined with a black minister from Beckley to anoint the site with water from the New River; local youth lit a candle for each departed soul. It had taken eighty-two years, but hopes ran high

that the workers' families might be reunited with
their loved ones across death.

Charlotte led me through an elegant archway, past
a stone engraved with the story of Hawk's Nest, and
up a short path to several neat rows of depressions,
each marked with a wooden cross and an orange
surveyor's flag. After days of rain, the depressions
held clear, still water that reminded me of baptismal
fonts in a church sanctuary. Hemlock, beech, and red
maple saplings grew among and inside them; moss
and ferns cushioned lichen-draped boulders forming
natural benches around the burials. Sunlight dappled
the glossy leaves of rhododendrons. It would have
been almost peaceful if not for the rushing traffic
above our heads. But it was beautiful, in spite of itself.

Later, as I sat in my car next to the creek that
drained Whippoorwill into the lake, I thought with
disgust: I swim here in the summer. Then I got a
random call from a friend who had lost the hard drive
that contained her life's digital history, who sought
my advice for its recovery. I told her that the thing
about data is it's not invisible; it's there, in traces.
Every byte has its physical form. Poetry, I remember
thinking, fills in the gaps.

Defense is sight; widen the lens and see
standing over the land myths of identity,
*   new signals, processes:*

The Gauley Bridge Historical Society is head-
quartered in some shambles in a narrow green
building on Route 60, next to a bridge that burned
twice in the Civil War. I had heard that the old
museum held documents relating to Hawk's Nest, so
I'd made an appointment to visit. It was raining when
I walked in, and Nancy Taylor sat at a desk among
empty display cases and stacks of files. She looked
at me like the public-school teacher she is and said,
"How can I help you?" in a tone that sounded like,
"Impress me." I told her I'd come to see the material
she mentioned on the phone, and she started
handing me bundles of papers.

I took them to a table and began flipping
through one of the stacks. I saw typewritten lists
of names, mortality tables, narratives, and I felt
the quickening of adrenaline through my blood.
I started urgently taking photos for later study,
but it soon became clear that the pages—which
appeared to be multiple sections of a single
text—were in jumbled disarray: faded legal-size
photocopies of names, some barely legible, and
hopelessly out of order. Under the tin roof in the
rain, I spent hours of the afternoon reconstructing
the document. Nancy seemed into it and said she
didn't have anything else to do. The chief of police
even dropped by to add his two cents. What he said,
I don't remember. All I could think about was the

sorting. Finally, I put the last of its two hundred and twenty-seven sheets into place, which turned out to be the title page: *Accident and Mortality Data on Rinehart and Dennis Company Employees and Miscellaneous Data on Silicosis,* Copy No. 2, March 10, 1936. Nancy and I cheered. She let me borrow the manuscript (I think she was grateful for the new order). I felt its preciousness in my hands, its presence in my car on the way to the copy shop.

When I finally read it, I could see it was the company's version of everything—their racially segregated tallies of employees who died in West Virginia from 1930 to 1935 (110 total); their count of "alleged" silicosis victims (fourteen); their estimation of the number of men they admit actually died of the disease (basically none). Line by line, they rebutted the testimony of the Gauley Bridge Committee's members, tearing into them with audaciously racist and belittling commentary, blaming the victims and "radical agitators" for all the trouble. Of their leader, George Robinson, they wrote that he was faking it all, in order to enjoy "notoriety, travel without cost to himself, and the pleasure of making an impression on white people for probably the first time." One section included a list of the deceased for whom H. C. White had served as undertaker: sixty-one employees (fifty-six black, five white) and five camp followers, including three women. He buried thirty-six at the

White Farm; the remainder were placed in other local cemeteries or shipped out of state to towns like Syria, Virginia; Union, South Carolina; Knoxville, Tennessee. . . . This list was flawed and, like the congressional hearing, not enough, but it was a beginning.

It was the beginning of more than memory. I'd found the company's narrative, yes, but it held the names, each one the beginning of a spell against the narrative of disaster. And against shame. Each one, a link to descendants for whom this list likely mattered a whole lot more than it did even to me. Here was the evidence one could intone. Like Rukeyser's poem, the list ran counter to the version of events where we all crawl off and die quietly. It held the potential to move that story, and it had been sitting here this whole time.

How had it made its way into this halfway shut-down museum? Nancy casually mentioned the name of a mutual acquaintance of ours who might know more about its origins, so I called him up. "I got [those materials] in a way that I probably shouldn't have," he told me. "I'll be real cryptic here. I was able to get into the rooms at the power station where they stored all the records, and I borrowed a lot of stuff one night, and I shared that with a number of folks. . . . And then I put the originals back." This was back in the 1980s. Apparently, he said, the company gathered every scrap of information they could about

the disaster and put it all in a room that "looked like
a jail cell," under the power house.

    and this our region,

desire, field, beginning.   Name and road,
communication to these many men,
as epilogue, seeds of unending love.

I used to be able to walk so close to the dam that I
could practically climb across it. At its edge sat a creepy
beige trailer with a single light that could be seen from
the gorge's rim at night. On a wet day in April, I set out
for it; I wanted to see the dam as it strained against
the spring rains. The river ran wicked under the
bridge where I parked and then started down a gravel
road thronged with red warning signs: EXTREME
DANGER—IF YOU NOTICE CHANGING
CONDITIONS, GET OUT!

    I had pushed levers called questions and the story
had opened. How unqualified, how unprepared I felt
for what I had found. Until that day at the Gauley
Bridge Historical Society, few words had adhered
to the uncounted dead, so I could abstract them in
the "supposed" or "alleged" past. Suddenly their scale
had become specific, and therefore vast. I knew their
families were out there, in my mind always some-
where south of here, living—either in full knowledge

of their family's inheritance, or in ignorance of it. Their trauma, I presumed, could be traced down through the generations. Yet none of this suffering was mine, was it? "Mine." I feared I was reinforcing some kind of savior narrative I had about my own white self—a middle-class woman who just wanted to "do the right thing," and not embarrass anybody, most especially herself. I worried that, instead of resurrecting, I had desecrated the resting dead—ghosts who had never elected me their spokesperson. The names of the Hawk's Nest dead gave me powers I wasn't sure I deserved.

Birds of prey called from the Appalachian jungle, and the purple bells of the paulownia trees rang out as I walked, listening for the dead. I turned to look behind me. I rattled my keys. What was I afraid of? The dam of history, bursting. I felt it cracking open, an inner chamber of the disaster that I hadn't known existed. I was afraid—of the woods, of the story, of the names.

I saw that a new barbed-wire gate had gone up to stop public access to the top of the dam, so I headed down a trail toward the river's edge, where waves dashed boulders like the starry backs of breaching whales. *These are roads to take,* Rukeyser wrote. I believed her. I took the roads. I thought of my country. And it had taken me to this terrible June, still looking to name what I'd found in the tunnel, for some cathartic shudder of light. The document *has* expanded, but into a longer list of undervalued, erased lives, as the rivers in West Virginia run their banks, as #WeAreOrlando and #BlackLivesMatter shout over and over to #SayTheirNames. Soon I will wake to #AltonSterling and #PhilandoCastile. Soon I will wake to Donald Trump's nomination for president. The same white supremacy that allowed, condoned, and covered up the mass killing at Hawk's Nest still asserts its dominance. The road of history is flooded with all of this, and so am I. But this is the road I must go down. It's the only one we have.

I drew closer to the water's rush and caught a view of the dam through the trees. I stopped and stared, and as I lifted my camera to record, I swear I heard the dam's steel gates groan. Those red signs flashed in my mind: KEEP AWAY! KEEP ALIVE! I ran scurrying back up the path. Circular clusters of fallen paulownia blossoms lit the way like lavender spotlights. With relief, I reached my car, and then I heard and felt a thunderous thump in the gorge behind me—something geological in scale fell. I thought of the blast from a surface mine, and then of my own beating heart.

EMPLOYEES OF RINEHART & DENNIS COMPANY
AND CAMP FOLLOWERS
WHO DIED IN WEST VIRGINIA
APRIL 1930–DECEMBER 1935

―――――――

This is a fraction of the Hawk's Nest dead—almost certainly, other victims' names were never recorded by the company, either because they died elsewhere or because their race meant they were written off. If disaster is the undoing of a star, then each of these names is a star being born. For more information, visit HawksNestNames.org.

NAME	AGE	RACE	PLACE OF BURIAL
Abraham, Eugene	21	B	White Farm, Summersville, WV
Adams, Winfred	—	B	Clairmont, NC
Alexander, James	32	B	Logan, WV
Allison, Robert	39	B	White Farm, Summersville, WV
Andrews, Sidney	22	B	Lewis Cemetery, Summersville, WV

NAME	AGE	RACE	PLACE OF BURIAL
Bales, Alonzo	24	B	Lewis Cemetery, Summersville, WV
Barrat/Barrett, Nathan	45	B	White Farm, Summersville, WV
Blakley, Thomas	—	B	Diamond, WV
Blankenship, Ballard	30	W	Lindsey, WV
Blankenship, Oran Mearl	41	W	Line Creek, WV
Bostic, Marshall	22	W	Elk View, WV
Bostic, (Mooney) Willie	16	B	Vanetta, WV
Bostic, Ray Ernest	28	W	Elk View, WV
Brown, James	26	B	White Farm, Summersville, WV
Brown, Parker	38	B	Potters Field, Fayetteville, WV
Brown, Walter Burley	21	W	Syria, VA
Browning, Fred	30	B	Summersville, WV
Burdette, Rufus	51	W	Poe, WV
Caldwell, Henry	30	B	Vanetta, WV
Cashion, Richard Wesley	48	W	Ansted, WV
Chambers, Benny	23	B	Lewis Cemetery, Summersville, WV
Chatfield, Fred	30	B	Vanetta, WV
Childers, Lewis B.	18	W	Dixie, WV
Clark, Nelson	30	B	White Farm, Summersville, WV
Cole, Lonnie C.	34	W	Jumping Branch, WV

NAME	AGE	RACE	PLACE OF BURIAL
Cooper, Mack	35	B	Lewis Cemetery, Summersville, WV
Cox, Milton	32	B	County Poor Farm
Daniel, A. L.	40	W	Atlanta, GA
Daugherty, George	35	B	White Farm, Summersville, WV
Devine, Henry	61	B	White Farm, Summersville, WV
Dickinson, Frans	42	W	Mt. Carbon, WV
Dixon, James	46	B	White Farm, Summersville, WV
Elders, Sylvia	35	B	White Farm, Summersville, WV
Euill, Gaston	36	B	Amherst, VA
Evans, H. C.	26	B	White Farm, Summersville, WV
Flack, Dewey	21	B	White Farm, Summersville, WV
German, Ben	38	B	Beckley, WV
Goines, Marvin	24	B	Not noted
Green, Clemon	28	B	White Farm, Summersville, WV
Haines, D. W.	34	W	Sunset Memorial Park, Charleston, WV
Hancock, Bennie H.	47	B	Hunter Cemetery, WV
Harvey, Calvin	38	B	White Farm, Summersville, WV
Hendrick, Henry (Harry)	42	W	Hendrick, WV
Hicks, James	42	B	Union, SC

NAME	AGE	RACE	PLACE OF BURIAL
Hockens (Hawkins), Richard	—	B	White Farm, Summersville, WV
Hunt, Thomas	45	B	White Farm, Summersville, WV
Inabinet, (S) Walter	27	W	St. Mathews, SC
Jackson, Whirley	24	B	Not noted
Jackson, Wm.	40	B	Summersville, WV
Johnson, Golden Allen	59	W	Gamoca, WV
Johnson, John	57	B	Boomer, WV
Johnson, Luther	—	B	White Farm, Summersville, WV
Johnson, Raymond	38	W	On Gauley, WV
Johnson, Robert	30	B	Vanetta, WV
Johnson, Walter	42	B	Prince, WV
Johnson, William	42	B	Montgomery, WV
Jones, Charley	52	W	Gamoca, WV
Jones, Charlie	52	B	Glen Ferris, WV
Jones, Cecil L.	23	W	Gamoca, WV
Jones, Lindsey	36	B	Vanetta, WV
Jones, Owen	22	W	Vanetta, WV
Jones, Robert	37	B	Not noted
Jones, Shirley	18	W	Gamoca, WV
Kincaid, Walter	59	W	Terry Cemetery, Victor, WV
Kube, A. L.	52	W	Roadsville, VA
Lane, Henry	26	B	Knoxville, TN
Lee, Sydney	33	B	Denmar, WV

NAME	AGE	RACE	PLACE OF BURIAL
Littlejohn, Mary	40	B	White Farm, Summersville, WV
Lyles, Ernest	23	B	Diamond, WV
McCalphin (McCalton), John	30	B	White Farm, Summersville, WV
McCrorey, George	31	B	Chester, SC
McDaniel, Clara	23	B	Glen Ferris, WV
McDaniel, Robert	50	B	Spring Hill, WV
McKeever, Grover	—	B	White Farm, Summersville, WV
McKission, James	30	B	White Farm, Summersville, WV
Means, Charles	21	B	Vanetta, WV
Miller, J. H.	—	B	White Farm, Summersville, WV
Mitchell, Fred	40	B	Rock Hill, SC
Monagan, John	35	B	Lewis Cemetery, Summersville, WV
Moore, James	47	B	White Farm, Summersville, WV
Morgan, Ellwood	42	B	Clanton, AL
Morrison, John	24	B	Summerlee, WV
Moses, Lona	25	B	Lancaster, SC
Murphy, Robert	46	B	Camden, SC
Murphy, Sam (Sim)	24	B	White Farm, Summersville, WV
Nelson, Alex.	44	B	White Farm, Summersville, WV
Nelson, George	44	B	Fayetteville, WV

NAME	AGE	RACE	PLACE OF BURIAL
Patterson, Charlie	25	B	Lewis Cemetery, Summersville, WV
Peyton, Arthur	—	W	—
Pickett, Willie T.	45	B	County Poor Farm
Potts, Jesse	73	B	Diamond, WV
Powell, Will	36	B	Mt. Holly, SC
Reed, Ernest	23	B	Lancaster, SC
Reed, W. M.	55	B	White Farm, Summersville, WV
Robinson, George	51	B	Vanetta, WV
Robinson, Will	60	B	Bayes Cemetery, Fayetteville, WV
Robinson, Willie	29	B	Summerlee, WV
Sandusky, Albert	49	B	Vanetta, WV
Saunders, Walter	40	B	Diamond, WV
Scott, Joe	45	B	Knoxville, TN
Shepherd, Howard	21	W	Gamoca, WV
Sherrod, John	—	B	White Farm, Summersville, WV
Singleton, Roosevelt	31	B	Lewis Cemetery, Summersville, WV
Skinner, C. M.	47	W	Thurmond, WV
Slaughter, Hudson	25	B	Pierce's Cemetery, Fayetteville, WV
Sloan, Mat	31	B	Vanetta, WV
Smith, Bee	29	B	Vanetta, WV
Smith, Frank	45	B	White Farm, Summersville, WV
Smith, H. L.	60	W	Mt. Holly, NC

NAME	AGE	RACE	PLACE OF BURIAL
Smith, John	28	B	High Springs, FL
Smoke, Emanuel	50	B	White Farm, Summersville, WV
Stokes, Willis	40	B	White Farm, Summersville, WV
Street, Lewis Walter	46	W	Swiss, WV
Stringer, Ralph	33	W	Cleveland, OH
Strong, John	37	B	White Farm, Summersville, WV
Sykes, Walter P.	24	W	Peachland, NC
Thompson, Enoch	—	B	White Farm, Summersville, WV
Ward, John	26	B	Kings Mt., NC
Ward, Sam	30	B	Vanetta, WV
Watkins, Sam	38	B	Vanetta, WV
Watts, W. A.	42	W	Not noted
White, James	—	B	Diamond, WV
Williams, Joe	30	B	Lewis Cemetery, Summersville, WV
Williams, Willie	—	B	White Farm, Summersville, WV
Wilson, James	32	B	Summerlee, WV
Woodard, Calvin	—	B	White Farm, Summersville, WV
Woods, Frank	23	B	White Farm, Summersville, WV
Woodward, Will	40	B	Lewis Cemetery, Summersville, WV
Yarber, George	18	W	Beckwith, WV

The Book of the Dead

Muriel Rukeyser

THE ROAD

These are roads to take when you think of your country
and interested bring down the maps again,
phoning the statistician, asking the dear friend,

reading the papers with morning inquiry.
Or when you sit at the wheel and your small light
chooses gas gauge and clock; and the headlights

indicate future of road, your wish pursuing
past the junction, the fork, the suburban station,
well-travelled six-lane highway planned for safety.

Past your tall central city's influence,
outside its body: traffic, penumbral crowds,
are centers removed and strong, fighting for good reason.

These roads will take you into your own country.
Select the mountains, follow rivers back,
travel the passes. Touch West Virginia where

the Midland Trail leaves the Virginia furnace,
iron Clifton Forge, Covington iron, goes down
into the wealthy valley, resorts, the chalk hotel.

Pillars and fairway; spa; White Sulphur Springs.
Airport. Gay blank rich faces wishing to add
history to ballrooms, tradition to the first tee.

The simple mountains, sheer, dark-graded with pine
in the sudden weather, wet outbreak of spring,
crosscut by snow, wind at the hill's shoulder.

The land is fierce here, steep, braced against snow,
rivers and spring. KING COAL HOTEL, Lookout,
and swinging the vicious bend, New River Gorge.

Now the photographer unpacks camera and case,
surveying the deep country, follows discovery
viewing on groundglass an inverted image.

John Marshall named the rock (steep pines, a drop
he reckoned in 1812, called) Marshall's Pillar,
but later, Hawk's Nest. Here is your road, tying

you to its meanings: gorge, boulder, precipice.
Telescoped down, the hard and stone-green river
cutting fast and direct into the town.

WEST VIRGINIA

They saw rivers flow west and hoped again.
Virginia speeding to another sea!
1671—Thomes Batts, Robert Fallam,
Thomas Wood, the Indian Perecute,
and an unnamed indentured English servant
followed the forest past blazed trees, pillars of God,
were the first whites emergent from the east.
They left a record to our heritage,
breaking of records. Hoped now for the sea,
For all mountaines have their descents about them,
waters, descending naturally, doe alwaies resort
unto the seas invironing those lands . . .
Yea, at home amongst the mountaines in England.

Coming where this road comes,
flat stones spilled water which the still pools fed.
Kanawha Falls, the rapids of the mind,
fast waters spilling west.

Found Indian fields, standing low cornstalks left,
learned three Mohetons planted them; found-land
farmland, the planted home, discovered!

War-born:
The battle at Point Pleasant, Cornstalk's tribes,
last stand, Fort Henry, a revolution won;
the granite SITE OF THE precursor EXECUTION
sabres, apostles OF JOHN BROWN LEADER OF THE
War's brilliant cloudy RAID AT HARPERS FERRY.
Floods, heavy wind this spring, the beaten land
blown high by wind, fought wars, forming a state,
a surf, frontier defines two fighting halves,
two hundred battles in the four years: troops
here in Gauley Bridge, Union headquarters, lines
bring in the military telegraph.
Wires over the gash of gorge and height of pine.

But it was always the water
the power flying deep

green rivers cut the rock
rapids boiled down,
a scene of power.

Done by the dead.
Discovery learned it.
And the living?

Live country filling west,
knotted the glassy rivers;
like valleys, opening mines,
coming to life.

STATEMENT: PHILIPPA ALLEN

—You like the State of West Virginia very much, do you not?

—I do very much, in the summertime.

—How much time have you spent in West Virginia?

—During the summer of 1934, when I was doing social work
down there, I first heard of what we were pleased to call
the Gauley tunnel tragedy, which involved about 2,000
men.

—What was their salary?

—It started at 40¢ and dropped to 25¢ an hour.

—You have met these people personally?

—I have talked to people; yes.

According to estimates of contractors
2,000 men were
  employed there
  period, about 2 years
  drilling, 3.75 miles of tunnel.
  To divert water (from New River)
  to a hydroelectric plant (at Gauley Junction).
The rock through which they were boring was of a high
 silica content.
In tunnel No. 1 it ran 97–99% pure silica.
The contractors
  knowing pure silica
  30 years' experience
  must have known danger for every man
neglected to provide the workmen with any safety
  device . . . .
—As a matter of fact, they originally intended to dig that
  tunnel a certain size?
—Yes.
—And then enlarged the size of the tunnel, due to the fact
  that they discovered silica and wanted to get it out?
—That is true for tunnel No. 1.
 The tunnel is part of a huge water-power project
   begun, latter part of 1929
   direction: New Kanawha Power Co.
    subsidiary of Union Carbide & Carbon Co.

That company—licensed:
to develop power for public sale.
Ostensibly it was to do that; but
(in reality) it was formed to sell all the power to
the Electro-Metallurgical Co.
subsidiary of Union Carbide & Carbon Co.
which by an act of the State legislature
was allowed to buy up
New Kanawha Power Co. in 1933.
—They were developing the power. What I am trying to
get at, Miss Allen, is, did they use this silica from the
tunnel; did they afterward sell it and use it in
commerce?
—They used it in the electro-processing of steel.
SiO_2 $\qquad$ SiO_2
The richest deposit.
Shipped on the C & O down to Alloy.
It was so pure that
$$SiO_2$$
they used it without refining.
—Where did you stay?
—I stayed at Cedar Grove. Some days I would have to hitch
into Charleston, other days to Gauley Bridge.
—You found the people of West Virginia very happy to pick
you up on the highway, did you not?
—Yes; they are delightfully obliging.

(All were bewildered. Again at Vanetta they are asking,
   "What can be done about this?")
 I feel that this investigation may help in some manner.
 I do hope it may.
 I am now making a very general statement as a beginning.
   There are many points that I should like to develop
   later, but I shall try to give you a general history of
   this condition first . . . .

GAULEY BRIDGE

Camera at the crossing sees the city
a street of wooden walls and empty windows,
the doors shut handless in the empty street,
and the deserted Negro standing on the corner.

The little boy runs with his dog
up the street to the bridge over the river where
nine men are mending road for the government.
He blurs the camera-glass fixed on the street.

Railway tracks here and many panes of glass
tin under light, the grey shine of towns and forests:
in the commercial hotel (Switzerland of America)
the owner is keeping his books behind the public glass.

Post office window, a hive of private boxes,
the hand of the man who withdraws, the woman who reaches
     her hand
and the tall coughing man stamping an envelope.

The bus station and the great pale buses stopping for food;
April-glass-tinted, the yellow-aproned waitress;
coast-to-coast schedule on the plateglass window.

The man on the street and the camera eye:
he leaves the doctor's office, slammed door, doom,
any town looks like this one-street town.

Glass, wood, and naked eye : the movie-house
closed for the afternoon frames posters streaked with rain,
advertise "Racing Luck" and "Hitch-Hike Lady."

Whistling, the train comes from a long way away,
slow, and the Negro watches it grow in the grey air,
the hotel man makes a note behind his potted palm.

Eyes of the tourist house, red-and-white filling station,
the eyes of the Negro, looking down the track,
hotel-man and hotel, cafeteria, camera.

And in the beerplace on the other sidewalk
always one's harsh night eyes over the beerglass
follow the waitress and the yellow apron.

The road flows over the bridge,
Gamoca pointer at the underpass,
opposite, Alloy, after a block of town.

What do you want—a cliff over a city?
A foreland, sloped to sea and overgrown with roses?
These people live here.

THE FACE OF THE DAM: VIVIAN JONES

On the hour he shuts the door and walks out of town;
he knows the place up the gorge where he can see
his locomotive rusted on the siding,
he sits and sees the river at his knee.

There, where the men crawl, landscaping the grounds
at the power-plant, he saw the blasts explode
the mouth of the tunnel that opened wider
when precious in the rock the white glass showed.

The old plantation-house (burned to the mud)
is a hill-acre of ground. The Negro woman throws
gay arches of water out from the front door.
It runs down, wild as grass, falls and flows.

On the quarter he remembers how they enlarged
the tunnel and the crews, finding the silica,
how the men came riding freights, got jobs here
and went into the tunnel-mouth to stay.

Never to be used, he thinks, never to spread its power,
jinx on the rock, curse on the power-plant,
hundreds breathed value, filled their lungs full of glass
(O the gay wind the clouds the many men).

On the half-hour he's at Hawk's Nest over the dam,
snow springs up as he reaches the great wall-face,
immense and pouring power, the mist of snow,
the fallen mist, the slope of water, glass.

O the gay snow the white dropped water, down,
all day the water rushes down its river,

unused, has done its death-work in the country,
proud gorge and festive water.

On the last quarter he pulls his heavy collar up,
feels in his pocket the picture of his girl,
touches for luck—he used to as he drove
after he left his engine; stamps in the deep snow.

And the snow clears and the dam stands in the gay weather,
O proud O white O water rolling down,
he turns and stamps this off his mind again
and on the hour walks again through town.

PRAISE OF THE COMMITTEE

These are the lines on which a committee is formed.
   Almost as soon as work was begun in the tunnel
   men began to die among dry drills. No masks.
   Most of them were not from this valley.
   The freights brought many every day from States
   all up and down the Atlantic seaboard
   and as far inland as Kentucky, Ohio.
   After the work the camps were closed or burned.
   The ambulance was going day and night,
   White's undertaking business thriving and
   his mother's cornfield put to a new use.

"Many of the shareholders at this meeting
were nervous about the division of the profits;
How much has the Company spent on lawsuits?
The man said $150,000. Special counsel:
I am familiar with the case. Not : one : cent.
'Terms of the contract. Master liable.'
No reply. Great corporation disowning men who made . . . ."
After the lawsuits had been instituted . . . .

The Committee is a true reflection of the will of the people.
Every man is ill. The women are not affected,
This is not a contagious disease. A medical commission,
Dr. Hughes, Dr. Hayhurst examined the chest
of Raymond Johnson, and Dr. Harless, a former
company doctor. But he saw too many die,
he has written his letter to Washington.

The Committee meets regularly, wherever it can.
Here are Mrs. Jones, three lost sons, husband sick,
Mrs. Leek, cook for the bus cafeteria,
the men : George Robinson, leader and voice,
four other Negroes (three drills, one camp-boy)
Blankenship, the thin friendly man, Peyton the engineer,
Juanita absent, the one outsider member.
Here in the noise, loud belts of the shoe-repair shop,
meeting around the stove beneath the one bulb hanging.
They come late in the day. Many come with them
who pack the hall, wait in the thorough dark.

This is a defense committee. Unfinished business:

Two rounds of lawsuits, 200 cases

Now as to the crooked lawyers

If the men had worn masks, their use would have involved

time every hour to wash the sponge at mouth.

Tunnel, 3$^{1/8}$ miles long. Much larger than

the Holland Tunnel or Pittsburgh's Liberty Tubes.

Total cost, say, $16,000,000.

This is the procedure of such a committee:

To consider the bill before the Senate.

To discuss relief.

    Active members may be cut off relief,

        16-mile walk to Fayetteville for cheque—

        WEST VIRGINIA RELIEF ADMINISTRATION, #22991,

        TO JOE HENIGAN, GAULEY BRIDGE, ONE AND 50/100,

        WINONA NATIONAL BANK. PAID FROM STATE FUNDS.

Unless the Defense Committee acts;

the *People's Press*, supporting this fight,

signed editorials, sent in funds.

Clothing for tunnel-workers.

    Rumored, that in the post-office

    parcels are intercepted.

    Suspected : Conley. Sheriff, hotelman,

    head of the town ring—

Company whispers. Spies,
　　The Racket.
　Resolved, resolved.
　George Robinson holds all their strength together:
　To fight the companies　　　to make somehow a future.

"At any rate, it is inadvisable to keep a community of dying
　persons intact."
"Senator Holt. Yes. This is the most barbarous example of
　industrial construction that ever happened in the world."
　Please proceed.
"In a very general way Hippocrates' *Epidemics* speaks
　　of the metal digger who breathes with difficulty,
　　having a pain and wan complexion.
　　Pliny, the elder . . . ."
"Present work of the Bureau of Mines . . . ."

　The dam's pure crystal slants upon the river.
　　A dark and noisy room, frozen two feet from stove.
　　The cough of habit. The sound of men in the hall
　　waiting for word.

　　　These men breathe hard
　　　but the committee has a voice of steel.

One climbs the hill on canes.
They have broken the hills and cracked the riches wide.

In this man's face
family leans out from two worlds of graves—
here is a room of eyes,
a single force looks out, reading our life.

Who stands over the river?
Whose feet go running in these rigid hills?
Who comes, warning the night,
shouting and young to waken our eyes?

Who runs through electric wires?
Who speaks down every road?
Their hands touched mastery; now they
demand an answer.

MEARL BLANKENSHIP

He stood against the stove
facing the fire—
Little warmth, no words,
loud machines.

Voted relief,
wished money mailed,
quietly under the crashing:

"I wake up choking, and my wife
rolls me over on my left side;
then I'm asleep in the dream I always see:
the tunnel choked
the dark wall coughing dust.

I have written a letter.
Send it to the city,
maybe to a paper
if it's all right."

Dear Sir, my name is Mearl Blankenship.
I have Worked for the rhinehart & Dennis Co
Many days & many nights
& it was so dusty you couldn't hardly see the lights.
I helped nip steel for the drills
& helped lay the track in the tunnel
& done lots of drilling near the mouth of the tunnell
& when the shots went off the boss said
If you are going to work Venture back
& the boss was Mr. Andrews

& now he is dead and gone
But I am still here
a lingering along

He stood against the rock
facing the river
grey river grey face
the rock mottled behind him
like X-ray plate enlarged
diffuse and stony
his face against the stone.

J C Dunbar said that I was the very picture of health
when I went to Work at that tunnel.
I have lost eighteen lbs on that Rheinhart ground
and expecting to loose my life
& no settlement yet & I have sued the Co. twice
But when the lawyers got a settlement
they didn't want to talk to me
But I didn't know whether they were sleepy or not.
I am a Married Man and have a family.   God
knows if they can do anything for me
it will be appreciated
if you can do anything for me
let me know soon

ABSALOM

I first discovered what was killing these men.
I had three sons who worked with their father in the tunnel:
Cecil, aged 23, Owen, aged 21, Shirley, aged 17.
They used to work in a coal mine, not steady work
for the mines were not going much of the time.
A power Co. foreman learned that we made home brew,
he formed a habit of dropping in evenings to drink,
persuading the boys and my husband—
give up their jobs and take this other work.
It would pay them better.
Shirley was my youngest son; the boy.
He went into the tunnel.

> My heart   my mother   my heart   my mother
> My heart   my coming into being.

My husband is not able to work.
He has it, according to the doctor.
We have been having a very hard time making a living since
    this trouble came to us.
I saw the dust in the bottom of the tub.
The boy worked there about eighteen months,
came home one evening with a shortness of breath.
He said, "Mother, I cannot get my breath."

Shirley was sick about three months.
I would carry him from his bed to the table,
from his bed to the porch, in my arms.

> *My heart is mine in the place of hearts,*
> *They gave me back my heart, it lies in me.*

When they took sick, right at the start, I saw a doctor.
I tried to get Dr. Harless to X-ray the boys.
He was the only man I had any confidence in,
the company doctor in the Kopper's mine,
but he would not see Shirley.
He did not know where his money was coming from.
I promised him half if he'd work to get compensation,
but even then he would not do anything.
I went on the road and begged the X-ray money,
the Charleston hospital made the lung pictures,
he took the case after the pictures were made.
And two or three doctors said the same thing.
The youngest boy did not get to go down there with me,
he lay and said, "Mother, when I die,
I want you to have them open me up and
see if that dust killed me.
Try to get compensation,

you will not have any way of making your living
when we are gone,
and the rest are going too."

>   *I have gained mastery over my heart*
>   *I have gained mastery over my two hands*
>   *I have gained mastery over the waters*
>   *I have gained mastery over the river.*

The case of my son was the first of the line of lawsuits.
They sent the lawyers down and the doctors down;
they closed the electric sockets in the camps.
There was Shirley, and Cecil, Jeffrey and Oren,
Raymond Johnson, Clev and Oscar Anders,
Frank Lynch, Henry Palf, Mr. Pitch, a foreman;
a slim fellow who carried steel with my boys,
his name was Darnell, I believe. There were many others,
the towns of Glen Ferris, Alloy, where the white rock lies,
six miles away; Vanetta, Gauley Bridge,
Gamoca, Lockwood, the gullies,
the whole valley is witness.
I hitchhike eighteen miles, they make checks out.
They asked me how I keep the cow on $2.
I said one week, feed for the cow, one week, the children's
        flour.

The oldest son was twenty-three.
The next son was twenty-one.
The youngest son was eighteen.
They called it pneumonia at first.
They would pronounce it fever.
Shirley asked that we try to find out.
That's how they learned what the trouble was.

> *I open out a way, they have covered my sky with crystal*
> *I come forth by day, I am born a second time,*
> *I force a way through, and I know the gate*
> *I shall journey over the earth among the living.*

> He shall not be diminished, never;
> I shall give a mouth to my son.

THE DISEASE

This is a lung disease. Silicate dust makes it.
The dust causing the growth of

This is the X-ray picture taken last April.
I would point out to you : these are the ribs;
this is the region of the breastbone;
this is the heart (a wide white shadow filled with blood).

In here of course is the swallowing tube, esophagus.
The windpipe. Spaces between the lungs.

Between the ribs?

Between the ribs. These are the collar bones.
Now, this lung's mottled, beginning, in these areas.
You'd say a snowstorm had struck the fellow's lungs.
About alike, that side and this side, top and bottom.
The first stage in this period in this case.

Let us have the second.

Come to the window again. Here is the heart.
More numerous nodules, thicker, see, in the upper lobes.
You will notice the increase : here, streaked fibrous tissue—

Indicating?

That indicates the progress in ten months' time.
And now, this year—short breathing, solid scars
even over the ribs, thick on both sides.
Blood vessels shut. Model conglomeration.

What stage?

Third stage. Each time I place my pencil point:
There and there and there, there, there.

   "It is growing worse every day. At night
   I get up to catch my breath. If I remained
   flat on my back I believe I would die."

   It gradually chokes off the air cells in the lungs?
   I am trying to say it the best I can.
   That is what happens, isn't it?
   A choking-off in the air cells?

Yes.
   There is difficulty in breathing.
Yes.
   And a painful cough?
Yes.

   Does silicosis cause death?

Yes, sir.

GEORGE ROBINSON: BLUES

Gauley Bridge is a good town for Negroes, they let us stand
    around, they let us stand
around on the sidewalks if we're black or brown.
Vanetta's over the trestle, and that's our town.

The hill makes breathing slow, slow breathing after you
    row the river,
and the graveyard's on the hill, cold in the springtime blow,
the graveyard's up on high, and the town is down below.

Did you ever bury thirty-five men in a place in back of your
    house,
thirty-five tunnel workers the doctors didn't attend,
died in the tunnel camps, under rocks, everywhere, world
    without end.

When a man said I feel poorly, for any reason, any weakness
    or such,
letting up when he couldn't keep going barely,
the Cap and company come and run him off the job surely.

I've put them
DOWN from the tunnel camps

to the graveyard on the hill,
tin-cans all about—it fixed them!—

TUNNELITIS
hold themselves up
at the side of a tree,
I can go right now
to that cemetery.

When the blast went off the boss would call out, Come, let's
    go back,
when that heavy loaded blast went white, Come, let's go back,
telling us hurry, hurry, into the falling rocks and muck.

The water they would bring had dust in it, our drinking
    water,
the camps and their groves were colored with the dust,
we cleaned our clothes in the groves, but we always had
    the dust.

Looked like somebody sprinkled flour all over the parks
    and groves,
it stayed and the rain couldn't wash it away and it twinkled
that white dust really looked pretty down around our ankles.

As dark as I am, when I came out at morning after the
    tunnel at night,
with a white man, nobody could have told which man was
    white.
The dust had covered us both, and the dust was white.

JUANITA TINSLEY

Even after the letters, there is work,
sweaters, the food, the shoes
and afternoon's quick dark

draws on the windowpane
my face, the shadowed hair,
the scattered papers fade.

Slow letters! I shall be
always—the stranger said
"To live stronger and free."

I know in America there are songs,
forgetful ballads to be sung,
but at home I see this wrong.

When I see my family house,
the gay gorge, the picture-books,
they raise the face of General Wise

aged by enemies, like faces
the stranger showed me in the town.
I saw that plain, and saw my place.

The scene of hope's ahead; look, April,
and next month with a softer wind,
maybe they'll rest upon their land,
and then maybe the happy song, and love,
a tall boy who was never in a tunnel.

THE DOCTORS

    —Tell the jury your name.

    —Emory R. Hayhurst.

    —State your education, Doctor, if you will.
      Don't be modest about it; just tell about it.

      High school Chicago 1899
      Univ. of Illinois 1903
      M.A. 1905, thesis on respiration
      P & S Chicago 1908

2 years' hospital training;
at Rush on occupational disease
director of clinic 2½ years.
Ph.D. Chicago 1916
Ohio Dept. of Health, 20 years as
consultant in occupational diseases.
Hygienist, U.S. Public Health Service
and Bureau of Mines
and Bureau of Standards

Danger begins at 25%
here was pure danger
Dept. of Mines
came in, was kept away.

Miner's phthisis, fibroid phthisis,
grinder's rot, potter's rot,
whatever it used to be called,
these men did not need to die.

—Is silicosis an occupational disease?
—It is.
—Did anyone show you the lungs of Cecil Jones?
—Yes, sir.

—Who was that?

—It was Dr. Harless.

"We talked to Dr. L. R. Harless, who had handled many of the cases, more than any other doctor there. At first Dr. Harless did not like to talk about the matter. He said he had been subjected to so much publicity. It appeared that the doctor thought he had been involved in too many of the court cases; but finally he opened up and told us about the matter."

—Did he impress you as one who thought this was a very serious thing in that section of the country?

"Yes, he did. I would say that Dr. Harless has probably become very self-conscious about this matter. I cannot say that he has retracted what he told me, but possibly he had been thrust into the limelight so much that he is more conservative now than when the matter was simply something of local interest."

Dear Sir: Due to illness of my wife and urgent professional duties, I am unable to appear as per your telegram.

> Situation exaggerated. Here are facts:
> We examined. 13 dead. 139 had some lung
> damage.
> 2 have died since, making 15 deaths.
> Press says 476 dead, 2,000 affected and doomed.

> I am at a loss to know where those figures were
> obtained.
>
> At this time, only a few cases here,
>
> and these only moderately affected.
>
> Last death occurred November, 1934.

It has been said that none of the men knew of the hazard connected with the work. This is not correct. Shortly after the work began many of these workers came to me complaining of chest conditions and I warned many of them of the dust hazard and advised them that continued work under these conditions would result in serious lung disease. Disregarding this warning many of the men continued at this work and later brought suit against their employer for damages.

While I am sure that many of these suits were based on meritorious grounds, I am also convinced that many others took advantage of this situation and made out of it nothing less than a racket.

In this letter I have endeavored to give you the facts which came under my observation . . . .

If I can supply further information . . . .

Mr. Marcantonio. A man may be examined a year after he has worked in a tunnel and not show a sign of silicosis, and yet the silicosis may develop later; is not that true?

—Yes, it may develop as many as ten years after.

Mr. Marcantonio. Even basing the statement on the figures, the doctor's claim that this is a racket is not justified?

—No; it would not seem to be justified.

Mr. Marcantonio. I should like to point out that Dr. Harless contradicts his "exaggeration" when he volunteers the following: "I warned many . . . ."

(Mr. Peyton. I do not know. Nobody knew the danger around there.)

Dr. Goldwater. First are the factors involving the individual.
Under the heading B, external causes.
Some of the factors which I have in mind—
those are the facts upon the blackboard,
the influencing and controlling factors.

Mr. Marcantonio. Those factors would bring about acute
silicosis?

Dr. Goldwater. I hope you are not provoked when I say "might."
Medicine has no hundred percent.
We speak of possibilities, have opinions.

Mr. Griswold. Doctors testify answering "yes" and "no."
Don't they?

Dr. Goldwater. Not by the choice of the doctor.

Mr. Griswold. But that is usual, isn't it?

Dr. Goldwater. They do not like to do that.
A man with a scientific point of view—

unfortunately there are doctors without that—
I do not mean to say all doctors are angels—
but most doctors avoid dogmatic statements.
avoid assiduously "always," "never."

Mr. Griswold. Best doctor I ever knew said "no" and "yes."
Dr. Goldwater. There are different opinions on that, too.
We were talking about acute silicosis.

The man in the white coat is the man on the hill,
the man with the clean hands is the man with the drill,
the man who answers "yes" lies still.

—Did you make an examination of those sets of lungs?
—I did.
—I wish you would tell the jury whether or not those lungs
   were silicotic.
—We object.
—Objection overruled.
—They were.

THE CORNFIELD

Error, disease, snow, sudden weather.
For those given to contemplation : this house,

wading in snow, its cracks are sealed with clay,
walls papered with print, newsprint repeating,
in-focus grey across the room, and squared
ads for a book : HEAVEN'S MY DESTINATION,
HEAVEN'S MY . . . HEAVEN . . . . THORNTON WILDER.
The long-faced man rises long-handed jams the door
tight against snow, long-boned, he shivers.
Contemplate.

                    Swear by the corn,
the found-land corn, those who like ritual. *He*
rides in a good car. They say blind corpses rode
with him in front, knees broken into angles,
head clamped ahead. Overalls. Affidavits.
He signs all papers. His office : where he sits.
feet on the stove, loaded trestles through door,
satin-lined, silk-lined, unlined, cheap,
The papers in the drawer. On the desk, photograph
H. C. White, Funeral Services (new car and eldest son);
tells about Negroes who got wet at work,
shot craps, drank and took cold, pneumonia, died.
Shows the sworn papers. Swear by the corn.
Pneumonia, pneumonia, pleurisy, t.b.

For those given to voyages : these roads
discover gullies, invade, Where does it go now?
Now turn upstream twenty-five yards. Now road again.
Ask the man on the road. Saying, That cornfield?
Over the second hill, through the gate,
watch for the dogs. Buried, five at a time,
pine boxes, Rinehart & Dennis paid him $55
a head for burying these men in plain pine boxes.
His mother is suing him : misuse of land.
George Robinson : I knew a man
who died at four in the morning at the camp.
At seven his wife took clothes to dress her dead
husband, and at the undertaker's
they told her the husband was already buried.
—Tell me this, the men with whom you are acquainted,
 the men who have this disease
 have been told that sooner or later they are going to die?
—Yes, sir.
—How does that seem to affect the majority of the people?
—It don't work on anything but their wind.
—Do they seem to be living in fear
 or do they wish to die?
—They are getting to breathe a little faster.

For those given to keeping their own garden:
Here is the cornfield, white and wired by thorns,
old cornstalks, snow, the planted home.
Stands bare against a line of farther field,
unmarked except for wood stakes, charred at tip,
few scratched and named (pencil or nail).
Washed-off. Under the mounds,
all the anonymous.
Abel America, calling from under the corn,
Earth, uncover my blood!
Did the undertaker know the man was married?
Uncover.
Do they seem to fear death?
Contemplate.
Does Mellon's ghost walk, povertied at last,
walking in furrows of corn, still sowing,
do apparitions come?
Voyage.
Think of your gardens. But here is corn to keep.
Marked pointed sticks to name the crop beneath.
Sowing is over, harvest is coming ripe.

—No, sir; they want to go on.
They want to live as long as they can.

ARTHUR PEYTON

Consumed. Eaten away. And love across the street.
I had a letter in the mail this morning
Dear Sir, . . . pleasure . . . enclosing herewith our check . . .
payable to you, for $21.59
     being one-half of the residue which
     we were able to collect in your behalf
     in regard to the above case.
In winding up the various suits,
     after collecting all we could,
     we find this balance due you.
With regards, we are
     Very truly,

After collecting

     the dust   the failure   the engineering corps
O love   consumed   eaten away   the foreman laughed
they wet the drills when the inspectors came
the moon blows glassy over our native river.

O love tell the committee that I know:
never repeat you mean to marry me.
In mines, the fans are large (2,000 men unmasked)
before his verdict the doctor asked me   How long

I said, Dr. Harless, tell me how long?
—Only never again tell me you'll marry me.
I watch how at the tables you all day
follow a line of clouds   the dance of drills,

and, love, the sky birds who crown the trees
the white white hills standing upon Alloy
—I charge negligence, all companies concerned—
two years O love two years he said he gave.

The swirl of river at the tidy house
the marble bank-face of the liquor store
I saw the Negroes driven with pick handles
on these other jobs I was not in tunnel work.

Between us, love
                                    the buses at the door
the long glass street   two years, my death to yours
my death upon your lips
my face becoming glass
strong challenged time making me win immortal
the love a mirror of our valley
our street   our river   a deadly glass to hold.
Now they are feeding me into a steel mill furnace
O love the stream of glass a stream of living fire.

ALLOY

This is the most audacious landscape. The gangster's
stance with his gun smoking and out is not so
vicious as this commercial field, its hill of glass.

Sloping as gracefully as thighs, the foothills
narrow to this, clouds over every town
finally indicate the stored destruction.

Crystalline hill: a blinded field of white
murdering snow, seamed by convergent tracks;
the travelling cranes reach for the silica.

And down the track, the overhead conveyor
slides on its cable to the feet of chimneys.
Smoke rises, not white enough, not so barbaric.

Here the severe flame speaks from the brick throat,
electric furnaces produce this precious, this clean,
annealing the crystals, fusing at last alloys.

Hottest for silicon, blast furnaces raise flames,
spill fire, spill steel, quench the new shape to freeze,
tempering it to perfected metal.

Forced through this crucible, a million men.
Above this pasture, the highway passes those
who curse the air, breathing their fear again.

The roaring flowers of the chimney-stacks
less poison, at their lips in fire, than this
dust that is blown from off the field of glass;

blows and will blow, rising over the mills,
crystallized and beyond the fierce corrosion
disintegrated angel on these hills.

POWER

The quick sun brings, exciting mountains warm,
gay on the landscapers and green designs,
miracle, yielding the sex up under all the skin,
until the entire body watches the scene with love,
sees perfect cliffs ranging until the river
cuts sheer, mapped far below in delicate track,
surprise of grace, the water running in the sun,
magnificent flower on the mouth, surprise
as lovers who look too long on the desired face
startle to find the remote flesh so warm.
A day of heat shed on the gorge, a brilliant
day when love sees the sun behind its man

and the disguised marvel under familiar skin.
Steel-bright, light-pointed, the narrow-waisted towers
lift their protective network, the straight, the accurate
flex of distinction, economy of gift,
gymnast, they poise their freight; god's generosity! give
their voltage low enough for towns to handle.
The power-house stands skin-white at the transmitters' side
over the rapids   the brilliance   the blind foam.

This is the midway between water and flame,
this is the road to take when you think of your country,
between the dam and the furnace, terminal.
The clean park, fan of wires, landscapers,
the stone approach. And seen beyond the door,
the man with the flashlight in his metal hall.
Here, the effective green, grey-toned and shining,
tall immense chamber of cylinders. Green,
the rich paint catches light from three-story windows,
arches of light vibrate erratic panels on
sides of curved steel. Man pockets flashlight,
useless, the brilliant floor casts tiled reflection up,
bland walls return it, circles pass it round.
Wheels, control panels, dials, the vassal instruments.
This is the engineer Jones, the blueprint man,
loving the place he designed, visiting it alone.
Another blood, no cousin to the town;

rings his heels on stone, pride follows his eyes,
"This is the place."

Four generators, smooth green, and squares of black,
floored-over space for a fifth.

                                        The stairs. Descend.
"They said I built the floor like the tiles of a bank,
I wanted the men who work here to be happy."
Light laughing on steel, the gay, the tall sun
given away; mottled; snow comes in clouds;
the iron steps go down as roads go down.

This is the second circle, world of inner shade,
hidden bulk of generators, governor shaft,
round gap of turbine pit. Flashlight, tool-panels,
heels beating on iron, cold of underground,
stairs, wire flooring, the voice's hollow cry.
This is the scroll, the volute case of night,
quick shadow and the empty galleries.

Go down; here are the outlets, butterfly valves
open from here, the tail-race, vault of steel,
the spiral staircase ending, last light in shaft.
"Gone," says the thin straight man.
"'Hail, holy light, offspring of Heav'n first-born,
'Or of th' Eternal Coeternal beam

'May I express thee unblamed?'"

And still go down.

Now ladder-mouth; and the precipitous fear,
 uncertain rungs down into after-night.
"This is the place. Away from this my life
 I am indeed Adam unparadiz'd.
 Some fools call this the Black Hole of Calcutta,
 I don't know how they ever get to Congress."

Gulfs, spirals, that the drunken ladder swings,
its rungs give, pliant, beneath the leaping heart.
Leaps twice at midnight. But a naked bulb
makes glare, turns paler, burns to dark again.
Brilliance begins, stutters. And comes upon
after the tail abstract, the ill, the unmasked men,
the independent figure of the welder
masked for his work; acts with unbearable flame.
His face is a cage of steel, the hands are covered,
points dazzle hot, fly from his writing torch,
brighten the face and hands marrying steel.
Says little, works : only : "A little down,
five men were killed in the widening of the tunnel."

Shell of bent metal; walking along an arc
the tube rounds up about your shoulders, black

circle, great circle, down infinite mountains rides,
echoes words, footsteps, testimonies.
"One said the air was thin Fifth-Avenue clean."
The iron pillars mark a valve division,
four tunnels merging.   Iron on iron resounds,
echoes along created gorges. "Sing,
test echoes, sing : Pilgrim," he cries.
singing *Once More, Dear Home*,
as all the light burns out.
Down the reverberate channels of the hills
the suns declare midnight, go down, cannot ascend,
no ladder back; see this, your eyes can ride through steel,
this is the river Death, diversion of power,
the root of tower and the tunnel's core,
this is the end.

THE DAM

All power is saved, having no end.   Rises
in the green season, in the sudden season
the white the budded

                        and the lost.
Water celebrates, yielding continually
sheeted and fast in its overfall
slips, down the rock, evades the pillars

building its colonnades, repairs
in stream and standing wave
retains its seaward green
broken by obstacle rock; falling, the water sheet
spouts, and the mind dances, excess of white.
White brilliant function of the land's disease.

Many-spanned, lighted, the crest leans under
concrete arches and the channelled hills,
turns in the gorge toward its release;
kinetic and controlled, the sluice
urging the hollow, the thunder,
the major climax

                    energy
total and open watercourse
praising the spillway, fiery glaze,
crackle of light, cleanest velocity
flooding, the moulded force.

> *I open out a way over the water*
> *I form a path between the Combatants:*
> *Grant that I sail down like a living bird,*
> *power over the fields and Pool of Fire.*
> *Phoenix, I sail over the phoenix world.*

Diverted water, the fern and fuming white
ascend in mist of continuous diffusion.
Rivers are turning inside their mountains,
streams line the stone, rest at the overflow
lake and in lanes of pliant color lie.
Blessing of this innumerable silver,
printed in silver, images of stone
walk on a screen of falling water
in film-silver in continual change
recurring colored, plunging with the wave.

Constellations of light, abundance of many rivers.
The sheeted island-cities, the white surf filling west,
the hope, fast water spilled where still pools fed.
Great power flying deep: between the rock and the sunset,
the caretaker's house and the steep abutment,
hypnotic water fallen and the tunnels under
the moist and fragile galleries of stone,
mile-long, under the wave. Whether snow fall,
the quick light fall, years of white cities fall,
flood that this valley built falls slipping down
the green turn in the river's green.
Steep gorge, the wedge of crystal in the sky.

How many feet of whirlpools?
What is a year in terms of falling water?
Cylinders; kilowatts; capacities.
Continuity: $\sum Q = 0$
Equations for falling water. The streaming motion.
The balance-sheet of energy that flows
passing along its infinite barrier.

It breaks the hills, cracking the riches wide,
runs through electric wires;
it comes, warning the night,
running among these rigid hills,
a single force to waken our eyes.

They poured the concrete and the columns stood,
laid bare the bedrock, set the cells of steel,
a dam for monument was what they hammered home.
Blasted, and stocks went up;
insured the base,
and limousines
wrote their own graphs upon
roadbed and lifeline.

Their hands touched mastery:
wait for defense, solid across the world.

Mr. Griswold. "A corporation is a body without a soul."

Mr. Dunn. When they were caught at it they resorted to the methods employed by gunmen, ordinary machine-gun racketeers. They cowardly tried to buy out the people who had the information on them.

Mr. Marcantonio. I agree that a racket has been practised, but the most damnable racketeering that I have ever known is the paying of a fee to the very attorney who represented these victims. That is the most outrageous racket that has ever come within my knowledge.

Miss Allen. Mr. Jesse J. Ricks, the president of the Union Carbide & Carbon Corporation, suggested that the stockholder had better take this question up in a private conference.

The dam is safe. A scene of power.

The dam is the father of the tunnel.

This is the valley's work, the white, the shining.

High	Low	Stock and Dividend in Dollars	Open	High	Low	Last	Net Chge.	Closing		
								Bid	Ask	Sales
111	61¼	Union Carbide (3.20) . . .	67¼	69½	67¼	69½	+3	69¼	69½	3,400

The dam is used when the tunnel is used.

The men and the water are never idle,

have definitions.

This is a perfect fluid, having no age nor hours,
surviving scarless, unaltered, loving rest,
willing to run forever to find its peace
in equal seas in currents of still glass.
Effects of friction : to fight and pass again,
learning its power, conquering boundaries,
able to rise blind in revolts of tide,
broken and sacrificed to flow resumed.
Collecting eternally power. Spender of power,
torn, never can be killed, speeded in filaments,
million, its power can rest and rise forever,
wait and be flexible. Be born again.
Nothing is lost, even among the wars,
imperfect flow, confusion of force.
It will rise. These are the phases of its face.
It knows its seasons, the waiting, the sudden. .
It changes. It does not die.

THE DISEASE: AFTER-EFFECTS

This is the life of a Congressman.
Now he is standing on the floor of the House,
the galleries full; raises his voice; presents the bill.
Legislative, the fanfare, greeting its heroes with
ringing of telephone bells preceding entrances,

snapshots (Grenz rays, recording structure) newsreels.
This is silent, and he proposes:

                              embargo on munitions

to Germany and Italy
as states at war with Spain.
He proposes
                    Congress memorialize
the governor of California : free Tom Mooney.
A bill for a TVA at Fort Peck Dam.
A bill to prevent industrial silicosis.

This is the gentleman from Montana.
—I'm a child, I'm leaning from a bedroom window,
clipping the rose that climbs upon the wall,
the tea roses, and the red roses,
one for a wound, another for disease,
remembrance for strikers. I was five, going on six,
my father on strike at the Anaconda mine;
they broke the Socialist mayor we had in Butte,
the sheriff (friendly), found their judge. Strike-broke.
Shot father. He died : wounds and his disease.
My father had silicosis.

Copper contains it, we find it in limestone,
sand quarries, sandstone, potteries, foundries,

granite, abrasives, blasting; many kinds of grinding,
plate, mining, and glass.

Widespread in trade, widespread in space!
Butte, Montana; Joplin, Missouri; the New York tunnels,
the Catskill Aqueduct. In over thirty States.
A disease worse than consumption.

Only eleven States have laws.
There are today one million potential victims.
500,000 Americans have silicosis now.
These are the proportions of a war.

>Pictures rise, foreign parades, the living faces,
>Asturian miners with my father's face,
>wounded and fighting, the men at Gauley bridge,
>my father's face enlarged; since now our house

>and all our meaning lies in this
>signature: power on a hill
>centered in its committees and its armies
>sources of anger, the mine of emphasis.

>No plan can ever lift us high enough
>to see forgetful countries underneath,

but always now the map and X-ray seem
resemblent pictures of one living breath
one country marked by error
and one air.

It sets up a gradual scar formation;
this increases, blocking all drainage from the lung,
eventually scars, blocking the blood supply,
and then they block the air passageways.
Shortness of breath,
pains around the chest,
he notices lack of vigor.

Bill blocked; investigation blocked.

These galleries produce their generations.
The Congressmen are restless, stare at the triple tier,
the flags, the ranks, the walnut foliage wall;
a row of empty seats, mask over a dead voice.
But over the country, a million look from work,
five hundred thousand stand.

THE BILL

The subcommittee submits:
Your committee held hearings, heard many witnesses; finds:

THAT the Hawk's Nest tunnel was constructed
  Dennis and Rinehart, Charlottesville, Va., for
  New Kanawha Power Co., subsidiary of
  Union Carbide & Carbon Co.

THAT a tunnel was drilled
  app. dist. 3.75 mis.
  to divert water (from New River)
  to hydroelectric plant (Gauley Junction).

THAT in most of the tunnel, drilled rock contained
  90—even 99 percent pure silica.

This is a fact that was known.

THAT silica is dangerous to lungs of human beings.
  When submitted to contact. Silicosis.

THAT the effects are well known.
  Disease incurable.
  Physical incapacity, cases fatal.

THAT the Bureau of Mines has warned for twenty years.

THAT prevention is: wet drilling, ventilation,
                              respirators, vacuum drills.
    Disregard : utter. Dust : collected. Visibility : low.
    Workmen left work, white with dust.
    Air system : inadequate.
    It was quite cloudy in there.
    When the drills were going, in all the smoke and dust,
    it seemed like a gang of airplanes going through
        that tunnel.
    Respirators, not furnished.
    I have seen men with masks, but simply on their
        breasts.
    I have seen two wear them.
    Drills : dry drilling, for speed, for saving.
    A fellow could drill three holes dry for one hole wet.
    They went so fast they didn't square at the top.
    Locomotives : gasoline. Suffering from monoxide gas.
    There have been men that fell in the tunnel. They had
        to be carried out.

The driving of the tunnel.
    It was begun, continued, completed, with gravest
      disregard.
    And the employees? Their health, lives, future?

Results and infection.

     Many died. Many are not yet dead.

     Of negligence. Wilful or inexcusable.

Further findings:

     Prevalence : many States, mine, tunnel operations.

     A greatest menace.

We suggest hearings be read.

     This is the dark. Lights strung up all the way.

     Depression; and, driven deeper in,

     by hunger, pistols, and despair,

     they took the tunnel.

Of the contracting firm

          P. H. Faulconer, Pres.

          E. J. Perkins, Vice-Pres.

     have declined to appear.

     They have no knowledge of deaths from silicosis.

     However, their firm paid claims.

     I want to point out that under the statute $500 or

        $1000, but no more, may be recovered.

We recommend.

     Bring them. Their books and records.

     Investigate. Require.

Can do no more.

     These citizens from many States

     paying the price for electric power,

     To Be Vindicated.

"If by their suffering and death they will have made a future
life safer for work beneath the earth, if they will have been
able to establish a new and greater regard for human life in
industry, their suffering may not have been in vain."

Respectfully,
Glenn Griswold
Chairman, Subcommittee
Vito Marcantonio
W. P. Lambertson
Matthew A. Dunn

The subcommittee subcommits.

Words on a monument.
Capitoline thunder. It cannot be enough.
The origin of storms is not in clouds,
our lightning strikes when the earth rises,
spillways free authentic power:
dead John Brown's body walking from a tunnel
to break the armored and concluded mind.

THE BOOK OF THE DEAD

These roads will take you into your own country.
Seasons and maps coming where this road comes
into a landscape mirrored in these men.

Past all your influences, your home river,
constellations of cities, mottoes of childhood,
parents and easy cures, war, all evasion's wishes.

What one word must never be said?
Dead, and these men fight off our dying,
cough in the theatres of the war.

What two things shall never be seen?
They : what we did. Enemy : what we mean.
This is a nation's scene and halfway house.

What three things can never be done?
Forget. Keep silent. Stand alone.
The hills of glass, the fatal brilliant plain.

The facts of war forced into actual grace.
Seasons and modern glory. Told in the histories,
            how first ships came

seeing on the Atlantic thirteen clouds
lining the west horizon with their white
            shining halations;

they conquered, throwing off impossible Europe—
could not be used to transform; created coast—
          breathed-in America.

See how they took the land, made after-life
fresh out of exile, planted the pioneer
          base and blockade,

pushed forests down in an implacable walk
west where new clouds lay at the desirable
          body of sunset;

taking the seaboard.   Replaced the isolation,
dropped cities where they stood, drew a tidewater
          frontier of Europe,

a moment, and another frontier held,
this land was planted home-land that we know.
          Ridge of discovery,

until we walk to windows, seeing America
lie in a photograph of power, widened
          before our forehead,

and still behind us falls another glory,
London unshaken, the long French road to Spain,
          the old Mediterranean

flashing new signals from the hero hills
near Barcelona, monuments and powers,
            parent defenses.

Before our face the broad and concrete west,
green ripened field, frontier pushed back like river
            controlled and dammed;

the flashing wheatfields, cities, lunar plains
grey in Nevada, the sane fantastic country
            sharp in the south,

liveoak, the hanging moss, a world of desert,
the dead, the lava, and the extreme arisen
            fountains of life,

the flourished land, peopled with watercourses
to California and the colored sea;
            sums of frontiers

and unmade boundaries of acts and poems,
the brilliant scene between the seas, and standing,
            this fact and this disease.

* * *

Half-memories absorb us, and our ritual world
carries its history in familiar eyes,
planted in flesh it signifies its music

in minds which turn to sleep and memory,
in music knowing all the shimmering names,
the spear, the castle, and the rose.

But planted in our flesh these valleys stand,
everywhere we begin to know the illness,
are forced up, and our times confirm us all.

In the museum life, centuries of ambition
yielded at last a fertilizing image:
the Carthaginian stone meaning a tall woman

carries in her two hands the book and cradled dove,
on her two thighs, wings folded from the waist
cross to her feet, a pointed human crown.

This valley is given to us like a glory.
To friends in the old world, and their lifting hands
that call for intercession.   Blow falling full in face.

All those whose childhood made learn skill to meet,
and art to see after the change of heart;
all the belligerents who know the world.

You standing over gorges, surveyors and planners,
you workers and hope of countries, first among powers;
you who give peace and bodily repose,

opening landscapes by grace, giving the marvel lowlands
physical peace, flooding old battlefields
with general brilliance, who best love your lives;

and you young, you who finishing the poem
wish new perfection and begin to make;
you men of fact, measure our times again.

* * *

These are our strength, who strike against history.
These whose corrupt cells owe their new styles of weakness
        to our diseases;

these carrying light for safety on their foreheads
descended deeper for richer faults of ore,
        drilling their death.

These touching radium and the luminous poison,
carried their death on their lips and with their warning
        glow in their graves.

These weave and their eyes water and rust away,
these stand at wheels until their brains corrode,
these farm and starve,

all these men cry their doom across the world,
meeting avoidable death, fight against madness,
find every war.

Are known as strikers, soldiers, pioneers,
fight on all new frontiers, are set in solid
lines of defense.

Defense is sight; widen the lens and see
standing over the land myths of identity,
new signals, processes:

Alloys begin : certain dominant metals.
Deliberate combines add new qualities,
sums of new uses.

Over the country, from islands of Maine fading,
Cape Sable fading south into the orange
detail of sunset,

new processes, new signals, new possession.
A name for all the conquests, prediction of victory
        deep in these powers.

Carry abroad the urgent need, the scene,
to photograph and to extend the voice,
        to speak this meaning.

Voices to speak to us directly.   As we move.
As we enrich, growing in larger motion,
        this word, this power.

Down coasts of taken countries, mastery,
discovery at one hand, and at the other
        frontiers and forests,

fanatic cruel legend at our back and
speeding ahead the red and open west,
        and this our region,

desire, field, beginning.   Name and road,
communication to these many men,
as epilogue, seeds of unending love.

ABOUT THE AUTHORS

MURIEL RUKEYSER (1913–1980) was a prolific American writer and political activist. In 1935 her first collection of poetry, *Theory of Flight*, won the Yale Younger Poets Prize, and she went on to publish twelve more volumes of poetry. She received a National Institute of Arts and Letters award, a Guggenheim Fellowship, the Levinson Prize for Poetry, and the Shelley Memorial Award, among other accolades. Rukeyser's writing consistently emphasized and utilized cinematic and graphic techniques, and she explored various connections between the visual and literary aspects of art. She originally intended *The Book of the Dead* to be published with multiple photos by Nancy Naumburg.

CATHERINE VENABLE MOORE is a writer in Fayette County, West Virginia. A graduate of Harvard University and the University of Montana, Moore is the recipient of fellowships from the MacDowell Colony, the West Virginia Humanities Council, and others. Her nonfiction has recently appeared in *Best American Essays*, *Oxford American*, *VICE*, and *Columbia Journalism Review*. She is also an honorary member of the United Mine Workers of America Local 1440. Currently, she is at work on a book of narrative nonfiction set in Appalachia, to be published by Random House.